Misery, Murder, Sex and Me: A Lighthearted Forensic Memoir

Dr. "Mad" Maddox Manson

Avicala Publications—Madison, WI
Paperback ISBN: 979-8-2185193-9-1
Library of Congress Control Number: 2024920297
Misery, Murder, Sex and Me: A Lighthearted Forensic Memoir
Author: Dr. "Mad" Maddox Manson
Digital distribution | 2024
Paperback | 2024

Photographs by Getty Images.

Published in the United States by New Book Authors Publishing

This book, although inspired by true events, is of a subjective and retrospective nature and as such aspects of it may be pseudohistorical. Biologically archived information, which is inherently reliant upon imperfect storage and recall, may not always be entirely factual. Moreover, all potentially identifying information has been deliberately anonymized. The reader is encouraged to read this book for informational, educational, and hopefully recreational purposes, but not necessarily to infer historical veracity. Any resemblance to any person living or dead may be construed as being coincidental, accidental, and/or circumstantial.

Dedication

For PAH, The Green Room Lady Extraordinaire

It is also dedicated to the many wretched souls whom I met as I made my living in the misery industry: those whose mistakes, misdeeds, and misshapen lives were tragic reminders of the futility of our grasping and delusion. It's a good thing that everything is impermanent!

Table of Contents

Prologue
Foreword is Forearmed

If I make it to the moon
I think I'll write a book
About the stupid things
I've done
And all the pain it took.
About the way I smiled
And then
I turned my back
And tossed my head
And lied and smiled again...

~Mad Manson, circa 1977

To symbolize their amazing superpowers and capacity to perform multiple tasks simultaneously, some Buddhist and Hindu deities are depicted with several pairs of arms. I admit to having but one pair of arms, and a similar number of hands. Nevertheless, in my days as a forensic psychologist I have often performed several distinct roles at the same time. And sometimes – at least from the perspective of the troubled people I have assessed for agencies such as the courts and the parole boards – I have wielded quite a bit of power.

Now, I am not necessarily the sort of person who has always been entirely comfortable with such power and responsibility, and therefore I have often relied on distraction, humor, and the very occasional small tumbler or two of tequila or bourbon to embolden and embalm me.

Although some may claim that I have a particular passion for a splash of Mexico's or Kentucky's finest tipples, it has also been asserted that wit and humor are conducive to a longer, happier, and altogether more palatable life. A sensitive funny bone is particularly important when practicing one of the 'darker' professions, such as morgue attendant, paramedic, pathologist, professional assassin or – murkiest of all – forensic psychologist.

Dealing as it does with forensic issues, some people may rightly perceive the meaty matter of this book to be quite dire and dreadful, delving into the most heinous human behavior and impulses imaginable: murdering someone for sexual gratification, for example, tends to be a uniquely human and, some might say, unfortunate activity.

Nevertheless, in these pages you will at times find a dash of levity to season the staider main course. Such uplifting and indeed lighthearted efforts at what I try to pass off as humor are offered in the belief that if we can't face death and destruction with spit on our lips, a chortle on our chops and a spring in our steps, we are headed for a very dark place. And just because we find ourselves surrounded by increasing chaos, madness, monsters, mobsters, mayhem, and death is no reason for us to become depressed!

It cannot be denied that we humans do some strange and sickly stuff. And that stuff can, and often does, inflict considerable damage on other sentient beings. However, the strangeness and sickness of it all, and the way in which it creates criminals and their crimes, can be the subject not only of study, but of moments of dark merriment and wonder. And if not exactly something at which to guffaw, quite possibly it can be something at which to gape in awe. For better or for worse, in sickness and in health, it's all a part of our weird humanity.

This book represents an eclectic and jaded glance over my shoulder at the thirty-plus years I have spent in the torrid trenches of torment known as the prisons, courts, probation offices, and clinics in which I have plied my trade. During my career I have interviewed, assessed, and authored mind-numbing reports on thousands of individuals who have been convicted of crimes ranging from murder to sexual assault to plotting to have one's spouse snuffed.

What has impressed me the most about my encounters with the offenders I've met is how interesting but perfectly ordinary many of those individuals were, and of how some of them would not have been seen as bad people had they not behaved so badly. Well, they wouldn't necessarily have been *terribly* bad people, had they not turned to crime as a means of meeting their needs and fulfilling their wishes. Of course, some of them were extraordinarily bad people.

Many of the fine folks I've evaluated and treated have been sex offenders: at the very beginning of my career, I accidentally stumbled into a one-year government contract to assess sex offenders, went on to inadvertently develop something of a reputation for being able to understand them and predict their behavior (I can't think why), and never again stumbled away. Despite being the lawbreakers, miscreants, and apparent perverts who are the most reviled by society (as well as by other criminals), I've found many sex offenders to be quite average people who wouldn't have been seen to be at all antisocial, and who wouldn't have come into contact with the criminal justice system, had it not been for their throbbing private parts and the bent brains that directed those parts.

Which I guess is another way of saying that sex offenders often would be quite decent people, were it not for their indecency. Which is why, when they are apprehended, those who have personally known the identified sex offender usually are quite surprised: alas, most sex offenders simply do not live up to their trench-coated, drooling, depraved and perennially horny stereotypes. But then again, a few of them do.

And the stuff that people do! Should I mention the guy who enjoyed having sex with a lingerie-adorned dead dog? Or the fellow who was startled to behold his victim's spirit leave her body after he had plunged a knife into her chest? Or the guy who had murdered his wife and three young children but had found God, forgiveness, and a sense of peace?

Or the high school teacher who very much enjoyed having sex with teenagers, including one of her students, but who righteously persisted in her belief that she had been judged unjustly? It is people such as these who provide fascinating and entertaining insight into the complexity and diversity of our human condition.

In these pages I will discuss some of those folks, talk a bit about their crimes, and share my idiosyncratic ideas about what made them tick and what inspired them to do what they did. I must admit, though, as I embark upon this confession, that the accounts provided are something like a stone skipping across the surface of my memory. I do not delve into some of the boring non-clinical stuff that I have done, such as training people like parole and police officers in risk assessment (I once ran a memorable day-long sex offender risk assessment training session for law enforcement personnel in a casino). Also, as a survival mechanism, I have forgotten or repressed many of the cases in which I have been involved. And sometimes I have omitted them from this account because I just don't consider them to be particularly interesting.

For instance, I don't talk about the young individual I saw a number of times in a jail who was transitioning from male to female, and who had long hair, fulsome breasts and (the person was undergoing hormone therapy but had yet to undergo surgery, and although referred to by the inmate, thankfully didn't exhibit it to me) a penis: he/she kept trying to show me his/her/their boobs, but after being involuntarily flashed the first time I was on high alert for any unauthorized mammary disclosure.

Nor do I mention the muscular, high-risk sex offender who'd recently been released from a federal jail, again was strolling the streets as a sex worker in the gay district and was exuding some seriously tough-guy machismo the first time we met – going so far as to brag about the perkiness and prodigious proportions of his pecker. But who was attired as a woman and was softly and demurely purring on about issues such as lingerie preferences during our chin wag a week later. Now, that is what I call a sudden transition and a fully fluid gender identity – either that or he was having a laugh.

I also leave out any reference to the Russian guy I assessed twice, a year or so apart, for his immigration lawyer: although he (and his alleged mother, who showed up for the first assessment) earnestly claimed that he worked in real estate, everything about him oozed Russian mafioso.

The impression of gangland involvement was reinforced when the role of his accompanying fiancé was played by two different, albeit equally accented and curvaceous, women during his two visits, both of whom were straight out of central casting for the part of a Russian prostitute – and both of whom professed their longstanding and undying love for him (did they all really think that I wouldn't spot the switch?). Memorable cases, but not remarkable enough to make the cut for this book!

So, the accounts that follow are off the top of my mind. But also, I hope like the cream off the top of the milk. And the narratives are as accurate as I can recall and convey. True, as noted above, the names may have been amended, and certain details may have been modified. But the tales are as true to life and death as they can be. Make of them, and the heroes and villains alive and dead and dying in these pages, what you will. And try to think kindly of those of us in the misery industries, tortured souls that we may be!

Chapter One
Hanging Around the Hoosegow
(Or How to Keep Your Head)

A forensic psychologist is a clinical psychologist who has undertaken the advanced training required to specialize in the evaluation, diagnosis and treatment of individuals who are involved with the criminal/justice/legal system.

To become licensed and to practice as a clinical psychologist, the aspiring shrink typically obtains an undergraduate degree, then goes on to acquire master's and doctoral degrees in the field of clinical psychology. Along the way the would-be psychologist will take various advanced courses related to normal and abnormal human psychology and behavior (in the first few weeks of my introductory psychopathology course in graduate school we were required to memorize the key diagnostic criteria for all the principal mental disorders and then pass an exam in order to qualify for proceeding with the course) as well as in associated areas such as biology, advanced statistics (huh?) and research design.

While partaking of such courses, the clinical graduate student is expected to conduct independent research and write two lengthy theses related to that research. In many of the larger and more reputable universities, such as the one in which I seem to vaguely recall having studied and trained, there are also major clinical comprehensive written and oral examinations that must be passed.

The professional psychologist's training process is arduous and is not for the faint of heart; it's far more difficult than most would expect. There were many sleepless nights (usually when completing the extremely enjoyable weekly take-home first-year statistics assignments, often completed in the wee hours of the morning). And oh yes, while taking the courses, conducting research, and drafting theses and dissertations, the student also must participate in a variety of clinical practicum placements and eventually complete a clinical residency.

When that's all done and dusted, the fresh graduate and potential psychologist sits a standardized comprehensive written examination for the professional practice of psychology: if that beast is defeated, and all of the other qualification ducks are in a row, the wannabe clinician goes on to take and hopefully pass the oral examinations that are set by the state/provincial licensing and regulatory colleges.

For a variety of reasons, only a minority of students gravitate toward forensic psychology, which requires additional training and experience in clinical areas related to the criminal and legal realms. The field of forensic psychology, which connects the clinical practice of psychology with the criminal justice system, and which tries to predict factors such as dangerousness and risk of re-offense, has been around in its present form for about 40 years.

I was drawn to the field because I tend to get bored easily and I've always had a passing interest in the macabre, murder, mayhem and machismo: sitting all day in an office and talking about feelings, desires, and neurotic impulses – or trying to cure patients of their anxiety, depression or fear of spiders – simply didn't hold the appeal of a world in which offenders and their close associates (lawyers, judges, and police officers) cavort. And oh yes, forensic psychology also tends to pay well. And finally, the forensic psychologist gets to chat with some seriously dark and fascinating people, some of whom you have heard or read about in the media.

In contrast, most forensic psychologists don't spend a great deal of time chewing the fat with each other. For several years I shared office space with a forensic psychologist who also served as something of a mentor to me during my early career, so from time to time I would chat with him.

Periodically, I'd also run into other psychologists at conferences and at various meetings, but being in independent practice I could go for quite some time without any meaningful contact with another psychologist. Now, although I must admit that I really did not miss seeing other psychologists, it has been noted that working in isolation can be personally as well as professionally damaging.

I do not doubt that such research is accurate, especially when the work in question is of a potentially disturbing nature. If you are a sensitive soul, because of the content of the reports to be read and types of people to be seen, forensic psychology can be a touch distressing. Even though I haven't felt a compelling need or desire to share my space or time with my professional colleagues, I'll be charitable and say that the loss was mine, not theirs.

I may well have become quite mad because of my relative isolation and the muck in which I've rolled. But madness alone can serve as an incredibly good form of defense, I think, and you must be a bit mad to want to be a forensic psychologist. I would be the last to know. But you will know after you've read this account.

Regardless, my own endeavors as a forensic psychologist began while I still had my clinical training wheels attached, when – being not yet fully qualified and still experiencing the wobbly challenges of my residency and practical training – as one component of my forensic rotation I was assigned to an old and woefully outdated prison. The jail in question had been upstanding since the late 1800s, and its main buildings had been left unaltered – and certainly unadorned and unimproved – since the grand old Victorian days.

The most ancient section of the jail, in which most of the inmates were held in barred cells that were arrayed on tiers, was quite monolithic and monstrous, like something out of movie set. You could almost hear the tin cups being scraped across the bars.

On my regular trips up and down the old concrete steps leading to the top floor of the main block, I had the pleasure of passing what once was the execution chamber.

Records indicate that between 1919 and 1959 some forty-four denizens of that den of iniquity checked out of the crowbar hotel by being hanged, most of them taking their last quick trip down a disused elevator shaft that had been thoughtfully repurposed for such speedy neck-stretching expeditions. (Back in the good old earlier days, they had simply hung the condemned out to die and dry in the prison courtyard.)

The last fellow to be executed at the joint was a guy who had, by his own swift confession, precipitously shucked off the mortal coil of his former male lover by stabbing him with a hunting knife. The erstwhile lover no longer had reciprocated the perpetrator's passion and commitment and had paid the ultimate price for such rejection. Although there are few things sleeker than a sharp knife blade, the course of true love it is said, does not run quite so smoothly.

Incidentally, by the late 1950s most condemned prisoners in the local geographic area were having their death sentences commuted to life imprisonment, and some historical sources suggest that this hombre had fallen victim to what are now popularly referred to as the 'homophobic' prejudices of the day.

Be that as it may, on the day of his judicially ordained demise the fellow supposedly had perished as normally as one can do, under such circumstances, by being, as officially stated, "executed according to the sentence imposed", dropping hard and fast and then being left to dangle for some twelve minutes, to ensure that he had been well and truly dispatched.

That said, and you my dear reader now having been fed the official line, I was reliably informed by one of the older physicians at the jail that things hadn't always gone quite so well. In fact, the old doc maintained that the final last drop hadn't gone exactly according to plan, and that the condemned had, quite literally (as opposed to just metaphorically), lost his head.

Although the dearly departed's death certificate asserts that the deceased suffered a "fracture dislocation of the cervical vertebrae" due to hanging, I don't suppose that it would be too much of a stretch to suspect that such a bland medical description would have been preferable to the more compelling, but possibly more accurate, medical term "avulsion" (which is an injury in which a body structure is torn off, either by trauma or surgery).

Even though a decent decapitation, however it's described medically, may be quite a thing to behold, and lately has been popularized by certain terrorist groups and an occasional middle eastern government, for the past few hundred years in the west it hasn't been viewed as a desirable outcome, at least when it comes to state-sanctioned executions.

So, how did such beheadings happen? Well, the usual suspect was the bane of modern western living: obesity. Between the time of the inmate's arrival at the jail and his expeditiously induced departure from this earth, he had little to do but sit around, eat, chew the fat (literally and figuratively), smoke, choke the odd chicken, and while away his remaining days as best he could.

Prison food (and yes, I've tried it) often being just a bit heavy on the carbs and fat, the inmates were inclined to gain weight during their incarceration. Sometimes quite a bit of weight. Even in the nineties I saw guys who were seriously slim and spry at the time of their admission to prison and who had metamorphosed into cheerily chubby and chunky chaps a year later.

The modern, and usually more humane, means of hanging someone is to employ something known as the measured drop. This is a process whereby the person's height and weight are used to calculate how long the rope should be, thereby ensuring a beautifully broken neck but neither a dangling choke nor a severed head. In the normal scheme of things this process wouldn't be rocket science, and at least theoretically it should be a snap to bring about the desired effect. Unfortunately, using the weight of the condemned prisoner at the time of his admission to the jail, rather than his weight after months, if not years, dedicated to the consumption of some seriously stodgy meals, didn't always result in anywhere near a precise estimate of the amount of rope needed.

Any such miscalculation could, and sometimes has, resulted in an abrupt separation or avulsion of head from body. That being the case, some of the local jailhouse hangers-on had got themselves decapitated upon their first and final speedy descent down the disused elevator shaft by which I serenely strolled.

A gallows room in an old prison – like the one by which the author strolled, but more roomy, warm, and welcoming

Incidentally, considering such botched and non-botched executions, and the massive amounts of anger, fear, frustration, and testosterone-laden energy which generally percolates inside any prison for men, it came as no surprise to me when I learned that the lands around the prison, which eventually was demolished early in the 1990s and replaced by some nice houses and a school, are reputed to have become home to a variety of ghostly emanations.

Seeing what I saw, and knowing what I knew, buying a home on the old prison grounds would have been at or close to the top of my "things not to do" list.

But as my dear Mrs. Manson said when she followed her accountant's advice to set up her own offshore bank account: to each their own. And I've devoted much of my life to the fact that ignorance truly is blissful. And thankfully, I wasn't living in or near the jail, I was merely attempting to work there. And my walk by the disused execution chamber was one which I undertook with nary a qualm – being as I was a cocky and relatively young guy.

More pressing on my mind, as I trudged up the steps to the top floor where I conducted my interviews of the prisoners, was who I was going to see and why I was going to see them. For indeed, in addition to a couple of hundred pigeons (even in a jail these were the flying kind of pigeon, not the stool kind: however, from what I saw, the flying pigeons certainly did manage to emit quite a lot of stool, which in some unused areas stood as mountainous monuments to their gastrointestinal systems and fecal incontinence), the uppermost floor of the building housed a special holding unit for remanded prisoners who, by virtue of their states of mind and/or their notoriety, required increased observation as well as segregation from the general inmate population.

Before launching into our discussion of the of the rakish upper floor residents, I should mention that there was quite a nasty riot in the cell block in which the special observation unit was housed, and that (although I deny having any responsibility for it) it occurred while I was working there.

Fortunately for me, it happened on one of my days off, and it was only upon my return that I witnessed its effects. I recall that during the riot a major concern had been that the rebellious and raucous general population prisoners would storm the upper floor observation unit, and that as a precaution the guards had locked down the unit in order to protect themselves and their charges from the hordes, anxiously awaiting the riot suppression cavalry from behind the thick steel door at the top of the steps.

In the days following the riot, the scene was quite something to behold. I can still remember walking through the barred inner gate – which had to be unlocked and relocked manually by a guard at each entrance and exit – and seeing the tiers of cells eerily emptied of their occupants. And devoid of just about everything else. The toilets and sinks lay broken upon the concrete floor, scattered hither and yon. Heaps of bedclothes and assorted other soiled garments, many of them singed by fire, were piled up everywhere.

Water from the broken plumbing fixtures trickled and gathered in pools. A fetid odor permeated the place: a pungent blend of dried milk and mold, ripened with the scent of dirty linen seasoned with a dash of old pee perfume. I remember thinking that the scene, which looked like something out of a movie or a scene from a popular TV series about zombies, served as a testament to the pent-up hostility of the inmates and the rage-fuelled damage that such a mob could inflict, given half a chance.

It takes but a tiny spark to ignite a large powder keg, and a lot of the guys in that jail had a whale of a lot of highly explosive emotions. During the riot, several inmates were injured either by other prisoners or guards, but no one was killed. It took a long time for the cell block to be returned to some semblance of normal – not that the place ever was normal, but let's just say that it was returned to its customary medieval mien.

The riot, and more significantly the media attention it garnered, expedited the demolition of the aging prison a few years later, leaving only the memories and the ghosts to linger in the shadows and to haunt the heads and hearts of those who lived and worked therein.

The tiers of cells in the prison's main building were stacked four stories high

Serial Killer Socializing

The more modern living unit or pod design was utilized at the remand center to which the author later consulted

But getting back to our conversation about the upper echelons of the prison, one special citizen who was held in the top-floor unit was a very notorious guy – let's call him Clint – who had derived perverse pleasure from the raping and killing of children. Clint had resided in the special observation unit during his pre-trial and trial days, just slightly before my time in the joint.

Although I didn't get to meet Clint, I did get to pass time with another equally charming fellow, by the name of Ken, who'd been charged with, and convicted of, first degree murder. Ken was a serial killer.

At the time of our encounter, Ken had been accused but not yet convicted of raping and killing a couple of young women, and he was sufficiently high-profile and special-needs to warrant confinement in the observation wing. And that was how, as a lowly and callow forensic psychologist trainee, I got to interview my first murderer. And a multiple murderer at that.

Go big or go home, I say.

And not only did I interview my first murderer: I got to do so all alone, without the presence or support of a more experienced clinician. And if that wasn't challenging enough, I even got to meet with Ken without any line-of-sight monitoring or immediate back-up from any guard, in a remote part of the upper floor of the prison, quite some distance from the living unit and the guard post. Locked behind a barred gate with Ken, with no guard within hailing or (saliva permitting) spitting distance, I chatted with my first serial murderer.

These days, when called upon to interview incarcerated offenders, clinicians routinely are assigned small personal protection alarms: one press of the big button will, at least in theory, bring the troops rushing heroically to one's rescue. In the institutions in which I more recently conducted assessments, I was under either video or direct line-of-sight observation by a guard while I was meeting with the inmate. And the government agency to which I last consulted required me to endure several hours of a violence prevention training workshop, with annual recurring training, as a condition of my contract.

But not back in the good old days, and especially not at the jail in which I got to shake the hand of my first murderer. There, most of the guards were burned-out ex-military types who for the most part clearly just didn't care.

This was the jail in which some guards were sanctioned after it was revealed that the doors to the main unit, which a few hundred inmates called home, had been left unlocked following a middle-of-the-night fast food run by one of the guards. (A sad but funny story. Fortunately, no one had escaped because the prisoners had remained locked in their cells and tucked beneath their blankets, blissfully oblivious of the fact that freedom had been brought so tantalizingly close while they'd slumbered. And to be fair, they would still have had to free themselves from their cells and tackle the razor-topped concrete perimeter walls, had they become aware of the unwitting open-door policy.)

But I digress. The thing was that, despite having been charged with more than one murder, Ken came across as a decent guy. He was somewhere in his early-to-mid-twenties, with long dark brown hair in the style of the day. He was quite well-spoken and of at least average intelligence.

Although I didn't conduct a formal assessment of Ken's personality or psychopathic traits (psychopathy being characterized by attributes such as selfishness, lack of empathy and remorse, callousness, manipulativeness, behavioural instability, and often glibness and superficial charm), in hindsight I suspect that Ken was right up there on the old psychopathy checklist scale. A heck of a nice guy until he didn't need or pretend to be.

As well as being closeted away with Ken the Kinky Killer, without any apparent monitoring or readily available assistance, two things were particularly memorable about my encounter with Ken. The first was that Ken had been assigned to some sort of work detail around the specialized holding unit, and therefore was wearing coveralls over his prison uniform.

At one point, in the midst of his discussion about how he was really a good guy who meant no harm to anyone (see above remark about superficial charm), he casually remarked that he had a screwdriver in his pocket and that if he had wanted to and had not been such a nice guy, he could have taken me out right there and then.

Which was indeed a very interesting and may I say insightful point for Ken to have made. I recall having murmured something sweetly banal in response, undoubtedly intended to keep both of us calm and alive. Being young, and having had some martial arts training (in hindsight, just enough to keep me unsafe) I didn't panic. But neither did I seek to provoke Ken ("oh yeah, well my screwdriver is bigger than your screwdriver") or unnecessarily prolong the interview.

The second memorable aspect of my conversation with Ken related to his stated recollections about his difficult relationship with his mother, who he said had suffered from bipolar disorder and had indulged in such unmaternal activities as pursuing him with scissors and threatening to (and trying to and/or wishing that she could) castrate him. And quite understandably, such formative experiences had left their mark on Ken's psyche and had helped to mold his attitudes toward others – females in particular, it would seem.

For me, Ken's account was quite edifying in that it afforded me a measure of insight into how some men who rape and commit other aggressive acts toward women come to think and behave as they do. That doesn't excuse or mitigate their behavior, of course, but it might help to explain the etiology of their decidedly misogynistic attitudes and actions – at least partially.

Regardless, what can be deduced from Ken's crimes – sexually assaulting and murdering young women – was that it's highly likely that he held some very negative views toward females. Moreover, it's often the case that for those who pair sex with murder or other acts of violence, the act of forcibly raping a female is very much connected with the perpetrator's need for dominance, control, revenge and aggression; the extreme and ultimate power play being the murder of the victim (and sometimes the way the victim's body is dispatched or even displayed).

In other cases, such as the one discussed later in which a little girl was killed, the murderer doesn't necessarily derive pleasure or satisfaction from the actual killing but does so more out of expedience. In still other instances, the murderer may be compelled or motivated by psychotic detachment from reality.

Speaking of such matters, criminologist Jennifer Chase (authorjenniferchase.com) has concluded that there are four primary types of serial killers, roughly divided into the categories of: a) power & control – deriving sexual gratification from dominating and degrading the victim; b) visionary – psychotic individuals who have visions or hear voices which direct them to kill; c) mission – those driven by a need or duty to kill certain classes of people, on the basis of their religious, racial, or occupational (think sex worker) affiliation; and d) hedonistic – those killers who get a sadistic thrill and sexual gratification from the kill, often incorporating elements of torture and mutilation of the victim into their murders.

Of course, there is bound to be quite a bit of overlap among these groups, and a few of the guys I've seen have fallen into three of the four categories (for example, killing prostitutes after dominating, humiliating, torturing and mutilating them.) But the divisions do appear to be reasonably accurate and descriptive.

Regarding the larger class of men who rape but don't murder, I should note that many if not most of the men who rape females – and here I'm talking about forcible sexual intercourse, not a situation in which a woman retrospectively alleges rape following a consensual sexual interaction – harbor pervasive feelings of hostility toward women.

They tend to view women as a class of individuals who simply cannot be trusted and toward whom they feel the need for domination and subjugation. Such attitudes may or may not extend to their deriving feelings of pleasure from inflicting pain and suffering upon females – or as noted above, the ultimate power trip of taking another person's life. In such cases, the paraphilia (sexual deviation) of sexual sadism also would apply.

More generally, and in keeping with the reality that a large part (there's also a biological component) of how we behave is based upon our past experiences, and how we've learned to act, many if not most males who do bad things to females are likely to have had negative encounters or other experiences with females early in their lives.

This is not a particularly popular concept today, given the preference by some to attribute the violence perpetrated by a subgroup of men to an inborn malevolent masculine trait, or alternatively to a partly learned but equally pervasive 'toxic masculinity' and misogyny. However, contrary to what such people would have you believe, and may themselves believe, extremes of aggressive behavior are enacted only by a small percentage of males. For the reader familiar with the statistical normal distribution curve, these are the guys who are on the tails of the distribution, therefore representing only a small fraction of all men.

Also, many of our behavioral tendencies are learned or socialized at any early age, when most children are increasingly and predominantly exposed to female influences in the home and school.

Setting aside such gender politics and polemics, an extreme example of a negative event which colored a boy's attitude toward females would be Ken's mentally troubled, castration-threatening mother. Less extreme examples may be real or perceived rejection or humiliation by girls in school, a distorted or difficult relationship with a female sibling or parent, and/or – and related to earlier experiences with females – an inability to perform sexually and/or socially in normal heterosexual associations.

Such experiences may or may not culminate in the development of a paraphilia related to rape, or they may result in the emergence of impotence or something completely different. For example, I recall one fellow who had a paraphilia for exhibitionism.

Delving into his background, it turned out that when he was approaching adolescence some of his peers had pushed him naked out of a locker room, thereby exposing him to a group of girls. Subsequently, the boy began to recollect and then fantasize about the experience, and to derive sexual arousal and masturbatory satisfaction from that fantasy. Over time, he progressed to re-enacting this fantasy, by creating situations in which he was able to wave his willy at unwitting and (usually) unwilling females.

Exhibitionism is only one of many paraphilias. Indeed, there are all kinds of paraphilias, and most of them don't involve sexual offending, unless the paraphilic behavior in question is directed toward a non-consenting person or animal. Every bird finds a bough upon which to perch and place its pecker.

And if paraphilias pique your interest, an internet search for "paraphilia" should furnish a veritable cornucopia of sexy information. Some noteworthy paraphilic favorites and recurring winners of the fictional but undoubtedly coveted "Paraphilia of the Year" award include necrophilia (corpses), zoophilia (animals), klismaphilia (enemas), and the perennial and all-time champions of the commode, coprophilia (feces) and urophilia (urine). But there are many, many more.

It's been a constant source of amazement, at least to me, to see how humans can become sexually fixated on – well, anything and everything.

And speaking of coprophilia (guaranteed as it is to generate a little excitement at otherwise dismal and dull social affairs): in the risk assessment training classes that I used to teach, very few of the attending professionals knew what the term meant. I suspect that more than a few of them thought that it had something to do with an erotic attraction to law enforcement officers (there being nothing quite like a person in uniform).

At such training sessions, I enjoyed proudly proclaiming that coprophilia is a "fondness for feces" or a "passion for poo," in recognition of the fact that some folks simply get off on the sight, sounds, smells and squishy sensations of the stuff. And what's not to like? Rekindling the delights and unrestrained relaxations of our placid pre-potty days!

All of which reminds me of a fellow I assessed circa 2010 whose sexual thing was to wear diapers. I can't recall whether feces featured in his diaper/baby clothing fetish, which is referred to in the clinical books as paraphilic infantilism or adult baby syndrome.

However, adult baby diaper lovers (ABDL) – who are not to be confused with those who are preferentially attracted sexually to children, who are pedophiles – can be roughly divided into those who derive sexual pleasure simply from dressing in diapers and role-playing an infant, and those who enjoy the sensation of defecating in their diapers. (Although this may seem like a minor distinction, it's a good thing to get settled fairly early in the dating relationship.)

What I've learned from interviewing those with paraphilias is that when it comes to sex, it's very much a case of "to each their own": sexual stimulation and gratification can be derived in an almost infinite number of ways, depending upon a person's biological and background experiences.

Although it can be tempting to deride or ridicule those with fetishes and paraphilias, provided that the behavior in question is consensual and private, and no one is getting hurt, I can think of no legitimate reason its practitioners should come to my or anyone else's professional attention. Weird is in the eye of the beholder. Sort of.

In fact, an argument could be made that at heart *all* sexual behavior is weird and irrational: two skeletons, surrounded by attached smelly internal organs and encased in fat and skin, engaged in a delicate copulatory act that frequently is balanced on a razor's edge of pleasure-pain/sensitivity-oversensitivity/let's do this again-don't ever call me again.

But the sex drive, although not essential to one's own survival, is necessary for our species' survival, and therefore is an extremely and extraordinarily compelling and demanding impulse, wet and wild and whacky or not.

And while we're discussing learned behaviors and the judgments of others, during my career I've come across some horrendous life histories. This has been particularly true with some of the more serious offenders who have committed acts such as murder and aggravated forms of assault and sexual assault.

Having reviewed many such histories, which sometimes have included both congenital physical and mental difficulties, often alongside pervasive and severe abuse that began in infancy, I've been left with the following question: If I'd been born into that person's body, with that person's brain, and had the same environmental experiences as that person, what exactly would have prevented me from turning out the same as that person?

Most of us like to believe that somehow, someway, we would have been different and better, and that for instance we wouldn't have run afoul of the law or otherwise behaved badly. However, I see no logical basis for this belief, unless we have faith in some sort of soul or core spirituality that would have made us different and would have set us apart from the bad guys, despite our biological and environmental experiences.

At the end of the day, apart from embracing a concept such as karma (our actions prior to as well as in this life influencing our current conditions and inclinations), or a belief in intrinsic evil, I have no meaningful answer to this question. Well, of course I do have my personal beliefs and hopes, but we'll leave a discussion of those for another day – or another life.

Anyway, getting back to Ken, I survived my encounter with him and his screwdriver – who, last I heard, was about thirty years into a life sentence and investing his time in the filing of various complaints – and I went on to see many more of his ilk, as well as an abundance of equally charming and misunderstood characters.

I interviewed many of those individuals in the old prison in which I'd chatted with Ken, because not long after I saw Ken I completed my training, graduated, passed my oral and written licensing exams, and became duly qualified for independent clinical practice. At that point I landed my first fully remunerated position, which was at – you guessed it – the same hoary old jail. Whether by accident or by design, the guests and ghosts at the gothic gaol weren't finished with me yet…

Most of the interesting characters in that prison were held in the top-floor special observation unit, so I used to conduct clinical rounds in that unit on each of the three days a week I spent at the facility. Not long after I began working there, Mrs. Manson partook of a guided tour of the jail, as a member of an excursion that periodically was provided for the spouses of the guards and other staff members. During the tour, the participants got to engage in such cheery and gratifying pastimes as being locked in a disused segregation cell.

Having survived such frivolity, when the tour group finally arrived on the top floor, Mrs. Manson recalls having gazed through an observation window and espying her husband interviewing a fellow who she later described as having borne an eery similarity to Charles Manson (no relation, I hasten to add) on an unmanageable hair day.

She was thoroughly impressed by the type of ruffian with whom her courageous spouse was cavorting, and I remain convinced that (although she's subsequently denied it) from that moment on and for at least the next couple of hours she held me in relatively high esteem – undoubtedly seeing me as the dashing, devil-may-care dude she once thought that she'd married!

Wife & Kiddies Killer Kibitzing

The exterior of an old state prison similar to the one haunted by the author

One fascinating fellow who did not look at all like Charlie Manson but who nevertheless was being held in the special observation unit was Ivan, a clean-cut but potentially overweight person whose path crossed mine shortly after I began to work at the old prison.

Ivan had been a fine, upstanding, and all-round unremarkable citizen until the fateful day on which he had decided that it would be a good idea to load a shotgun, point the open end in the direction of his wife and young children, and repeatedly pull the trigger. In doing so, Ivan had expeditiously and unceremoniously dispatched his family into the hereafter and thereby had acquired the status of grieving widower, former father, and current inmate.

Ensuing from this ebullient burst of familial activity, Ivan had found himself in the unfamiliar and unenviable position of being locked up in the big house, facing several murder charges. Immediately after his transfer from police custody to pretrial prison detention, Ivan's perplexity and panic regarding his newfound circumstances impelled him to proclaim that he'd swallowed something sharp, thus imperiling his life.

Alas, at a nearby hospital he was deemed not to be in any immediate danger, and much to his dismay he was promptly chauffeured back to the old pokey. Given the nature of his charges, his lack of jailhouse experience and his forlorn personality, Ivan was placed in the special observation unit. He was quite a dependent personality who seemed to tolerate the unit remarkably well – which was a good thing, because it was to be his home for the next few years.

As such, although Ivan eventually pled guilty to his charges and was transferred to a federal penitentiary in which to serve out a life sentence, during pre-trial and trial he was held in the same observation unit that Ken the Killer (aka Screwdriver) had called home. The unit in question was quite primitive by contemporary standards, boasting as it did two sets of six open-fronted, barred cells. Each cell was generously furnished with a slender mattress on its lush concrete floor, a dainty sink on one wall, and a state-of-the art "honey bucket" (for pee and poo) in one corner.

Although not much by today's luxury hotel standards, this unit quickly assumed the comforts of home for Ivan. In fact, it became so comfortable and familiar for him that he was extremely nervous when it came time for him to leave it behind after he'd been sentenced and classified to a federal joint.

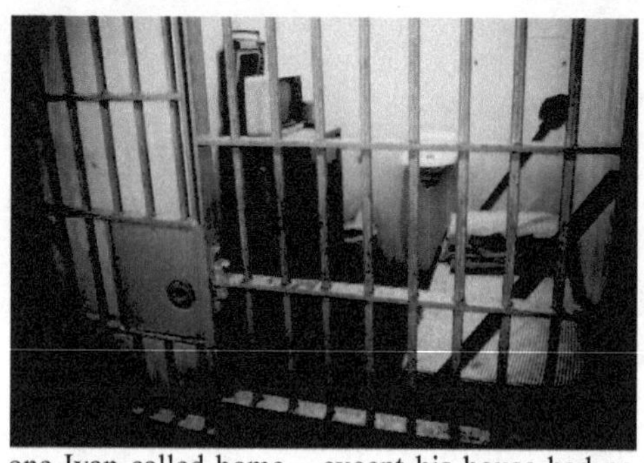

A cozy cell like the one Ivan called home – except his house had no toilet or furnishings and his mattress was on the floor

Because in his heart of hearts, although he could wield a mean shotgun Ivan was a timid sort of guy. Undoubtedly self-focused, and demonstrably capable of murderous emotion and motion, he lacked personal resilience. He was the kind of guy who may have been a bit of a bully in school but who was fundamentally insecure, needy, and pusillanimous.

The killing of his wife and children having been indicative of his pitiful inability to cope with whatever personal circumstances were plaguing him at the time (most likely difficulties with and rejection by his wife, with the associated realization that he was about to lose his family and his world as he knew it).

Ivan's use of the shotgun, as far as I could determine during my numerous conversations with him, was the result of an angry, desperate, despondent, dependent, revengeful, overwrought, and self-defeating response to his eroded marital circumstances. At least by his account – and I believe it to have been true – his original intention had been to dispatch his wife and children and then to turn the firearm upon himself to join them at the pearly gates.

The trouble being that he'd lost his nerve when it came time to shoot himself. Without the capacity to pull the trigger as he'd gazed down the dark and hollow end of the still-smouldering shotgun, he'd been quickly apprehended and incarcerated. And now he was here, sitting before me and chatting away like he'd known me forever.

Ivan was genuinely distressed by what he'd done (which is not to be confused with the regret, experienced by many offenders, at having been caught and punished for what they'd done), although it was difficult to establish the relative amounts of remorse about his actions versus his sorrow about his situation.

Also, I do recall him having struggled a bit with his explanation to the court about how, during the throes of an impulsive and unpremeditated act, he'd managed to methodically reload the shotgun and persevere with the slaughter of his family. There were depths to Ivan and his ability to commit such horrendous behavior that fortunately are beyond the ken of most of us, including me – whose job it is to try to make sense of such events. I try, but nobody (especially Mrs. Manson) ever said that I'm perfect or omniscient.

Despite such complexity, before long Ivan simplified his undoubtedly torturous and convoluted emotions by converting to a fundamental religion, which significantly helped him to deal with the darkness of his deeds and the dungeonlike dankness of his digs: Indeed, Ivan became a Bible-carrying born-again Christian.

One of the more alluring and magnanimous aspects of fundamental Christianity being that, if one is contrite about one's sins and accepting of Jesus and the basic tenets of the religion, it offers a wholesale blanket of forgiveness for one's misdeeds.

As such, it was a perfect fit for Ivan, affording him the opportunity to lessen his psychic pain in the belief that although he'd sinned mightily by slaughtering his wife and children, he'd been (spiritually) absolved of his sins and, being born again, no longer was the person he'd been when he'd killed his family. And as a value-added bonus, Ivan could expect to be re-united with his family when, as a reborn and saved soul, he went to meet his Maker: at which time the conversation would be a remarkably interesting one.

I like to think that Ivan's religious beliefs have been a source of comfort for him during the decades that he's been incarcerated since we last met. This was one of the more tragic cases I've seen, in which a few minutes of Ivan being consumed and overwhelmed by his negative emotions (superimposed, of course, upon his intrinsic capacity to kill those human beings who presumably had been closest to him and for whom he'd once cared) had catalyzed a cascade of events that had terminated three lives and had irrevocably changed the course and quality of what remained of his own life.

The last time I checked, 12 years ago, Ivan was diligently serving his sentence. He became institutionalized very quickly, and I expect that he got along relatively well in the protective custody unit of the federal prison to which he was sent. (Protective custody, or PC, is where inmates who would be at risk in the general population are placed. Sex offenders and others whose personality and/or offenses meant that they would not do well in the larger inmate group, usually wind up in PC.)

However, I don't really know what happened to Ivan or how he's been doing because, like most of the individuals I've had the pleasure of meeting professionally, I've had no way of following up on him. Well, I suppose that I could have followed up and even visited him if I'd really tried but, you know…

I have been asked what it has been like to have done my best work with the guys I've seen, to have offered my best advice to or (more often) about them, and then not to know what happened to them and how their fates had unfurled. Well, as with certain other aspects of my life, I've been blessed (cursed?) with the capacity to be unaffected by such ignorance: I was paid to get the job done – usually to assess someone and to provide a report – and that's what I did.

In the main, I didn't develop any strong attachment to the people I was assessing or seeing for a few sessions, and I moved on without too much of an afterthought. For better or for worse, I had little or no desire to track down the people I saw to explore what happened to them – although sometimes I did find out from other professionals who subsequently were supervising or managing them.

However, there have been some exceptions to my general disinterest in knowing what happened to the people I saw. Toward the end of my career, the primary exceptions to my profound lack of curiosity arose when I was asked to carry out assessments for immigration lawyers, who wanted to know not only how much of a risk Mr. or Ms. X posed to society, and therefore whether they represented a reasonable candidate for criminal rehabilitation and/or a stay of deportation, but how the family members would be affected by their removal from the country.

When conducting such evaluations, I met some of the most normal and pleasant people I have encountered and found myself being touched by the plight of innocent family members. I've wondered how some of those cases evolved.

Otherwise, apart from contemplating whether certain dangerous individuals I've assessed were back on the streets and whether (particularly if I've written something about them that they wouldn't like, which often was the case) they were likely to show up while I was outside mowing the lawn or painting the house, I really haven't worried or wondered too much about most of the offenders I've met.

Call it callousness or self-protective detachment, but a touch of psychopathy really can be helpful when working in a profession in which darkness and hurt pervade. And yet, as I've grown older the armor has thinned and rusted, and I've become a restless and inconsistent sleeper....

At Home on the Range

But to return for a few moments to the old prison – where my duties included not only assessments (primarily to monitor and reduce the risk of inmates inflicting harm upon themselves or others) but also "treatment" or, more accurately, quite basic, short-term supportive counselling – I interviewed a whole lot of men.

Sex offenders, assaulters, murderers, and thieves sat before me, and we engaged in amicable discourse. Most of those conversations now are lost in the mists of time, but a few remain quite vivid in my mind.

I remember interviewing a former pro football star (I used to go to the home games and cheer him on) who'd fallen on hard times after his retirement from football, and who didn't look quite as good in his inmate coveralls as he had only a few years earlier in his team colors, loping into the end zone with the ball in his arms.

I told him that he was a great athlete (which was true) who I'd very much enjoyed watching play. To which he accurately but sadly replied "I used to be." A combination of a drug habit and an inability to manage momentary fame and fortune had contributed to his downfall.

I also had a good chat or two with an erstwhile globe-trotting reporter whose enjoyment of the hardships, excitement, and adrenalin rush from being in the world's combat zones and other hot spots had stood him in good stead during his stay in the cells. He'd seen it all, and he freely acknowledged to me that he'd thrived on the danger and variety that had spiced his life.

I recall him smiling and saying, in response to my standard questions about the quality of his sleep and appetite, that he was eating and sleeping well and in fact always was able to "sleep the sleep of the unjust." Some folks just don't worry too much – which can be a good thing when taken in moderation, but not so good when the anxiety and worry levels get too low for the person's own good.

However, one young guy whose anxiety levels certainly were not low when I first saw him was new to the adult prison system; understandably enough, he was quite frightened by his circumstances. (The sign over the door to the prison admissions area reassuringly announced: "This Is It: You've Hit Rock Bottom.")

In particular, the guy was scared about the very real possibility of him being subjected to physical, sexual, and/or psychological abuse in the prison wing – such wings being known colloquially as "ranges" – to which he'd been assigned. I attempted, as best I could, to calm his fears and to assure him that all would be well, even if I didn't completely believe it myself. I remember having made a call to his unit supervisor, to alert the staff to the kid's worries and try to ensure that he'd settle in as safely as possible.

But lo and behold, when the guy was called to my office for a follow-up visit a few days later, I was taken aback by his changed demeanor. Gone was the simpering, fearful and effeminate felon, and now sitting before me was a calm, contented, and cocky con. As we chatted, he assured me that his problems were behind him and that he'd settled into his new digs quite nicely, thanks very much.

He assured me that he no longer needed to see me, and I assumed that he'd found one or more guardians on his living unit, who in exchange for 'friendship with benefits' (sexual relations), were protecting him from the other inmates. A case fit to be closed, with all the involved players apparently having reached a mutually agreeable arrangement. To the best of my knowledge, I never saw the guy again.

Several years later, Fred, who was the manager of the prison section in which the above felon had been a resident, and who had wielded considerable local authority and autonomy within that sector, was convicted of a variety of offenses, in particular sexual ones.

All the offenses were related to his place of work. It seems that in exchange for sexual favors from some of the younger inmates in the prison wing over which he had authority, Fred had furnished them with protection and other special considerations. Strangely, he'd never bothered to mention such arrangements and goings-on to me during our periodic work meetings, although it later emerged that a number of the guards who had worked directly with Fred had been concerned and suspicious about some of his shenanigans.

Fred was a different sort of fellow, rusty of hair and face, prone to pudge, and in my estimation harboring a variety of psychological conflicts, including deeply seated feelings of insecurity and inferiority in response to which he had developed over-compensatory power needs.

He wasn't suffering from any sort of diagnosable personality or mental disorder, but there was something a bit odd and off-putting about him. He'd worked his way up from being a uniformed prison guard to a middle manager with some authority, and as a bonus he'd got to wear a jacket and tie. He impressed as being a touch inept, a bit of a bully, and as having a need to prove himself. He also tended to be something of a talker, and although I didn't see him that often, usually when we met his conversations revolved around him, his opinions, and his accomplishments.

Several years after my departure from the old jail, and not having had any contact at all with Fred during the intervening time, we were re-united when he was referred to me for an assessment at a specialized probation/parole office to which I was consulting. By then, Fred had been convicted, had served his time, and now was on parole. His supervising officer was seeking my opinion concerning Fred's psychological status and recidivistic (re-offense) risk, as well as his case management needs.

Considering the circumstances of our meeting and our former working relationship, I found my encounter with Fred to be a bit awkward. However, judging by his congenial and quite hearty presentation, Fred was unfazed – or at least able to fake it well, summoning even more of his usual bluster and bravado. I strongly suspect that beneath his brash front Fred was extremely mortified at being in the role of interviewee, obliged to answer my questions in completely different circumstances and with quite an altered power dynamic than the one we'd previously enjoyed.

His way of dealing with these dramatically changed fortunes, and with his probable discomfort was to put on a 'hail fellow well met' persona and to greet me like a long-lost colleague, rather than an assessing psychologist. Of course, it's also quite possible that there was a part of Fred that was impervious to the immense embarrassment that most of us would have experienced in such a situation, and it's likely that such distortions of thinking and feeling had played a causal role in his precipitous downfall from prison authority to prisoner and then parolee.

Although I doubt that Fred has relapsed sexually or subsequently committed any other illegal acts (even at that time he was already middle-aged and at heart quite a law-and-order type), he did end up having more historical charges laid against him in connection with his abuse of power, and as a result he served even more time.

He's also been the subject of civil litigation in the form of lawsuits from former inmates. I find myself pondering the mindset of someone who thought that he could engage in the type of behavior that resulted in his disgrace and downfall, particularly playing with a cast of characters who weren't exactly known for their loyalty and high ethical standards – and who certainly weren't above extortion, "ratting someone out" and/or seeking compensatory damages for real or alleged mistreatment and trauma.

Still, (as my dear mom used to say, after she'd figured out who her son was turning into) it takes all kinds, and were it not for such kinds, my job wouldn't have been as entertaining or rewarding.

As something of an aside, but still regarding prison guards, throughout the years I've encountered many female correctional officers who were working in men's prisons. These days, you're as likely to run into women working in male jails as you are men working there. Conversely, I have never seen a male guard working in a female prison.

I know that, at least when I was actively consulting to the regional and federal correctional systems, men were strongly discouraged, rejected, or downright forbidden from applying to work as a correctional officer in a women's jail.

The obvious rationale for this double standard is easy to identify. Statistically and historically, males are much more likely to be sexually abusive or exploitative of women than women are of men.

For this and other reasons, the risk of male guard/female prisoner interactive problems was too high to justify the employment of males as guards of females. Indeed, when I was a rookie psychologist I was once warned by a senior female nurse that female inmates tend to be particularly manipulative and exploitative of any guys who come into their orbit, and that any visits that I might make to a female jail were to be undertaken with the utmost caution and vigilance.

I'd venture to say that nowadays such a warning would hold tenfold, and that it would indeed take a cavalier male clinician to enter such an environment without ensuring that he was carefully chaperoned throughout his visit.

Indeed, these days, given the ease with which very public allegations of abuse are being routinely leveled against males, I'd undertake a professional visit to a women's prison only with considerable forethought and assurance that I would be under constant monitoring while doing so: one accusation of misconduct, however unsubstantiated, can ruin your day and your career. (The inner rapper in me might croon that "the smear becomes a spear, despite a later clear.")

Prisoners have a lot of time on their hands and have been known to take pleasure in initiating lawsuits and a variety of other anti-authority complaints against guards, prison food, and, well, everything.

For example, several years ago, the federal government was sued by a former inmate on the grounds that the felonious fellow had resumed his use of heroin following his release from federal custody. Pared to the bone, the guy's argument went along the lines that he'd been released prematurely from prison, his early release had made him more likely to resume his heroin habit, and therefore someone (certainly not him!) was to blame, and he deserved a lot of money to ease his pain and suffering.

Because I'd seen him a few times while he was on parole to monitor him and try to ease his transition back into the community, and because I was obliged to carry a whack of malpractice insurance, I was named as a co-defendant in the lawsuit. Although the complaint ended up being dismissed before it went to trial, and there wasn't any sort of financial negotiation or settlement, it exemplifies the kinds of often frivolous complaints and claims that are leveled by some inmates, especially those who languish long-term in our federal facilities.

More recently, when I conducted a court-ordered psychological assessment of a female inmate who was in her early thirties, I did so via video conference – not only saving me a long drive out to the holding facility but avoiding any potential misunderstanding or difficulties. (Although video conferencing has become a popular means of conducting prison interviews, whenever possible I prefer an in-person interview in which you can get a better sense of the individual by interacting directly with them, watching their eyes, and sometimes even smelling them.)

The woman was awaiting sentencing on charges related to child abduction and various other charges which signified that she was more than capable of malice and mendacity. In a subsequent conversation with the woman who was prosecuting the case, I was informed that in fact the defendant was highly manipulative and coquettish and had indulged in alluring and luring behaviour such as gently laying her hand on a male courtroom guard's arm. Especially because my report on the woman didn't cast her in a particularly flattering light, I thought that it was a good thing that I'd listened my instincts and had avoided unnecessarily being alone with her. Sadly, such are the days in which we live.

But getting back to the many women working in men's prisons: what would motivate a young female to seek a career in a prison in which all the inmates are male? And how can we justify the fact that, in these days of gender equity and equality, women are permitted intimate access to male prisoners, whereas men aren't allowed a similar level of access to female prisoners?

Well, I don't have an answer for the second part of that question, but my response to the first part would be that in my experience many male and female correctional officers aspired to be police officers, and that although working as a prison guard may be perceived by some as falling lower on the enforcement hierarchy, it's within the ballpark. Also, a percentage of female correctional officers are themselves more inclined toward traditionally masculine interests: I haven't inquired (nor would I ever in a million years do so) about their personal proclivities, but I assume that owing to their individual aptitudes, motivations and dispositions, a vocation in a masculine milieu, in a role that carries a degree of authority, would be a good fit for them.

On the other hand, some female prison guards in men's jails are motivated primarily by the offer of steady, good-paying employment in what usually is a government position, with its perquisites and pensions.

In my experience, such women often are inclined to leave front-line correctional work quite early in their careers, burning out and/or gravitating toward positions (such as working in the reception or visits areas) that remove them from the hubbub, disharmony and danger of daily, close contact with a group of high-testosterone males. Still other female guards – well, I have my suspicions that some of them, either consciously or unconsciously, enjoy being in extremely near, intimate proximity to the males who are under their watchful eyes, and that gaining access to them doing all sorts of things in private settings is not entirely anathema to them.

I'll leave it to the reader's imagination as to what sorts of situations might exist in environments in which the correctional officers are required to constantly look into the inmates' cells and monitor changing areas and showers.

That said, I must add that I've seldom ventured into the cell tiers and living units, and that my only personal experience with a female guard exploiting, or at least taking advantage of, her position, was a woman in her late twenties who was working in the admissions area at a pretrial center.

She took a particularly resolute interest in frisking the men as they entered the facility, conducting a very thorough examination of their thigh and "oh me, oh my" areas – only to ensure that they were carrying no weapons or contraband, of course…

You be the judge. I will just say that such invasions of privacy never would be tolerated were the gender roles to be reversed, and that indeed some male inmates have voiced their strong opposition to women being permitted or even encouraged to actively supervise male prisoners and have access to them in their very personal spaces. Further, in comparison with the general community, a higher-than-average percentage of inmates are likely to have experienced abuse during their formative years.

So, it's safe to say that the inmates' negative reaction to invasive circumstances may well intensify any underlying anger and resentment that they may have, especially toward women. Which I suppose in a backwards sort of way could be construed as a good thing, helping to keep the anger pot boiling, and ensuring continued job security for the jail guards and prison psychologists.

For just as there would be no need for law enforcement officers were it not for those who break the law, so there would be no need for correctional officers, were it not for those in need of correction!

Chapter Two
Doing The Time for Sex & Crime

Although my work in the hoary hoosegow made for a good foot in the door of my forensic career and made for quite an intriguing and sometimes entertaining gig for a rookie forensic psychologist – in some ways helping to better prepare me for forensic work than my formal training had done – it had never been my desire or intention to remain there for long.

Too oppressive an environment and too burned-out in the old guard department. And so, as soon as I'd become sufficiently established professionally, I exfiltrated myself from the prison and spread my wings in the direction of private practice, picking up contracts for probation and parole consulting and various other steamy realms of clinical and forensic assessment and treatment along the way.

And so I began to regularly visit the maximum- and medium-security federal prisons that peppered the landscape surrounding (remote enough to be out of sight and mind to most gentle and good urban citizens but close enough to be accessible) the large metropolis in which I was based. It was during such visits that I encountered many of the most dangerous and fascinating felons, initially by virtue of a contract I was offered to psychologically evaluate parole applicants.

The same contract also required me to assess inmates' levels of risk and overall quality of functioning in whatever institution they were being housed. Parole boards being the curious creatures that they are, or are supposed to be, were keen to know what I had to say about the degree of peril posed by the guys who were seeking parole. The prisons on the other hand primarily were interested in learning how best to case manage their inmates, and to determine an inmate's capacity and suitability for rehabilitation, work release programs, and transfer to lower security.

It's a safe bet that most people wouldn't want to spend a great deal of time in even the most modern prison. By definition, except for the minimum-security institutions that look and function much like work camps, prisons are, how should I put it, confining. It takes some mental adjustment to accommodate the fact that you can't just get up, stretch and yawn, and saunter out the door when the spirit moves you.

Although I'm not particularly prone to claustrophobia or panic, I can still recall the feelings of uneasiness I experienced during my early training days, locked as I was behind the impenetrable steel doors of the inmate reception area in the basement of a pretrial detention center: the reality that I couldn't just stroll outside and suck in a breath of fresh air whenever I so desired required some psychological processing.

However, after a few months such confinement became entirely familiar to me, and after that I seldom gave the matter a second thought. The mind is an amazing creature, adjusting as it usually does to even the most difficult, weird, and onerous circumstances.

Although the difficulty of getting out of the prisons didn't noticeably change during my years of gracing their corridors, getting into the higher security correctional institutions certainly became more difficult.

In the halcyon days of the eighties and early nineties, I'd usually book an appointment to assess an inmate (a process which wasn't overly difficult unless it was an assessment for the defense, in which case it became a bit more challenging), show up, show my ID, maybe pass through a rudimentary metal detector, and wander inwards.

As time went on, metal detectors and X-ray machines became standard fare, and then automated drug detection equipment at the main entrance was introduced. A professional visitor who is going to be interacting with an inmate also must be issued a personal protection alarm and a visitor's badge. You can't bring in cell phones, USB sticks or similar items. Most recently, I was advised that my keys had to be locked away prior to entry.

Allow an extra 15 to 20 minutes to park in the visitor's area, saunter over to the entrance, and humbly undergo the "please may I come into your nice jail?" routine.

For good reason, the process of gaining access to the maximum-security federal jail, where pistol-packing guards were responsible for initial security screening, was the most complicated. First, I would have to pass through the gatehouse, which was really a large stand-alone room that straddled the outer perimeter fence and housed the screening machinery and the clipboard-carrying guards.

In that area I would do my absolute best to assure the stone-faced guardians that I was who I was (even though at one time in my career I was going in and out of there every couple of weeks) and that I was on official business. I would be required to sign in – noting the date, time, person to be visited, and the purpose of the visit.

Confident that I was who I said I was and was not up to no good or casual sightseeing, the door of the gatehouse which led inward would be unlocked electronically so that I could sashay into the empty wasteland that lay between the inner and outer fences. I'd then follow a short path to the main prison building, and usually as I reached its door the gatehouse guard would open it remotely so that I could penetrate and enter the inner sanctum.

Once thus situated, I'd pass through a barred gate, again remotely operated by a guard in a control room near the building entrance (the gate sliding silently to the side as it opened and closed), to gain access to the administrative area.

Although the main building of the max security prison housed several offices, including the psychology unit, I would usually have to wander farther afield to see the guy I'd arranged to meet. To do that, I would pass through another barred gate and proceed from the main building into the central courtyard. Located around the courtyard were the various cell units: general population, protective custody, and segregation.

There were also various other units or service areas peppered around the courtyard, such as the prison kitchen. A complaint I heard from the protective custody inmates was that the meals were prepared by general population inmates, who loved to hate the lowly pc skinners (sex offenders) and rats (informants) and would vent their venom by spitting and secreting other bodily fluids into the meals that were to be distributed in the pc unit.

Such comestible considerations aside, by the time I began to conduct assessments at the major federal joints, I was used to being tucked away behind several layers of locked gates and thick concrete walls.

I was, as they say, doing good time. Inured to the manure. And getting paid more than the few bucks a day that most of the inmates could expect to reap as recompense for their work within the barbed wired walls. Even so, I found the milieu in which I conducted some of my most heavy-duty evaluations, deep within the bowels of the maximum-security facility in which the most dangerous offenders were housed, to be seriously oppressive and demoralizing.

A solitary confinement cell block

The most tightly-contained and overpowering area into which I had the pleasure of poking my proboscis was the segregation/special holding unit of the regional maximum-security prison mentioned above, within which inmates remained locked in their cells most of the time – typically for 23.5 out of 24 hours.

The denizens of this depressing unit had no interaction with other inmates while they were in their cells, and walked or otherwise exercised in a small, approximately 20 x 30-foot room located near the center of the unit, which was itself surrounded by its own concrete walls and crowned with a wire fence ceiling. A maximum of three inmates were permitted to exercise together at any one time in this area, affording them a brief opportunity to gossip, share recipes, and catch up on soap opera trivia.

In this forlorn segregation unit, there were probably at least a half-dozen barriers between me and (and the inmates' and the guards') freedom, and I could hardly wait to complete an assessment and get out of that concrete catacomb.

It therefore came as something of a relief when this stalwart shrink would step swiftly out of the windowless, artificially-illuminated confines of the maximum-security segregation facility – or even the more spacious and swish protective custody and general population units – into the central courtyard around which the prison buildings were arrayed. The only trouble being that to leave the jail proper I had to cross this expansive yard, by myself, carrying nothing but my trusty briefcase and my dubious attitude.

Adding to my concerns was the fact that by the time I'd finished an evaluation it was usually around noon – by which point, especially during the warmer months, the courtyard was teeming with inmates.

And quite a number of those inmates were burly young guys with tattoos and muscles that glistened and rippled as a testament to the significant amounts of time they worked the weights. And a lot of those inmates were violent and dangerous: that was why they were being housed in a maximum-security prison.

Now, I'd had the honor of meeting a number of those fine fellows and sharing my undoubtedly keen opinions about them in my reports. In doing so, I hadn't always had overly positive things to say about them. And although I've always tried to report some of the person's more positive attributes, it wasn't unusual for the overall tone of my assessment reports to be quite negative.

From an inmate's perspective, my findings often would not have been conducive to their mission to expedite their release or get whatever else it was that they were hoping to get. Many times, quite the opposite.

I'm sure that it won't come as a surprise to you that criminals aren't always the most introspective and self-aware citizens. There is a tendency for a hefty percentage of them to lay the blame for their problems everywhere else apart from on their own doorstep. Often, they commit crime because they can't think, or can't be bothered to think, of more legitimate and arduous ways to make a living.

As such, they aren't necessarily inclined to respond with sweetness and aplomb when their foibles and faults are pointed out to them. A readiness to "shoot (or more of a concern to me in the prison courtyard, stab) the messenger" certainly was not beyond the realms of possibility and my vivid imagination.

My identified role of being just such a messenger therefore was front and foremost in my mind as I meandered merrily through the prison yard. It is indeed perfectly possible that occasionally during such strolls the thought that I was potentially in mortal danger had rumbled its way through my subconscious mind.

Certainly, the ever-vigilant guards high atop the perimeter walls were armed with carbine rifles. They were perfectly safe up there, and I was happy for them and their families. I've no doubt that they had spent quite some time at the nearby shooting range, had passed some sort of marksmanship qualification, and if prompted would have been quite willing to spread the lead: two to the thoracic cavity, followed by a head shot if required, and all that.

Nonetheless, for some strange reason the knowledge that an aggrieved inmate who had decided to play a game of Shank the Shrink ("shank" being prison slang for a knife or the act of stabbing someone) could have been shot or otherwise reprimanded, offered me scant comfort. I therefore walked briskly and earnestly through the yard, assuming what I believed was my most fearsome but serenely self-assured gait and a "don't mess with this psycho psych" expression. I'm guessing that such defensive techniques were successful, inasmuch as I remained unsullied and un-shanked, and was never even verbally accosted.

As real as such issues and threats were in my mind at the time, they were all in my mind. And I have been known to wander into Farmer Paranoia's chicken coop from time to time. So maybe the guys in that courtyard were the closest thing that I'll have to being my best friends forever, and I was just being hypervigilant and silly. Indeed, Mrs. Manson periodically reminds me of an incident that occurred around that time, when we were strolling downtown and she had suddenly gripped my arm, startled and frightened by the unexpected approach of a scary and seedy guy.

However, the fine fellow had smiled broadly and exclaimed "Hi, Dr. Manson" – being pleased to see a familiar face following his recent release from custody. You just never know whose life you've touched, however lightly and momentarily. And truth be told, life is an adventure and I guess that if I'd wanted boring, I could have stayed in my office and declined to dip my toes in the jailhouse waters.

Such heartwarming reflections aside, despite my survival in the max security prison's courtyard, the entire scenario represented a major vulnerability in terms of the safety and security of that institution. I and other contractors or employees could easily have been swarmed by the inmates.

Moreover, such glaring gaps in security were by no means unique to that facility. At every federal prison that I've visited – and there have been many, ranging from low-to-maximum-security – at various points I've had to walk unescorted past inmates within the grounds of the institution. Looking back, I'm a bit surprised that I was never involved in some sort of confrontation or incident, even of a minor nature.

I can recall no specific publicized event in which an inmate waylaid a member of the public on prison grounds. However, several years ago at a nearby medium-security facility that I often visited, an irritated inmate repeatedly stabbed and killed the prison's female librarian. The guy had been having a difficult day and had decided to make the librarian's day even worse.

Such incidents underscore the point that no work in which you're exposed to potentially and historically violent individuals is entirely risk-free, especially when you're dealing with fundamentally damaged people who may have been exposed to quite a bit of violence in their lives.

Or who simply find themselves in dire psychological or personal circumstances, with a rage burning in their hearts and a belief that they have nothing to lose by giving vent to their fury. Or who simply lose control and revert to type. Although it's best not to be the spark that lights the fuse that ignites the dynamite, sometimes your luck just runs out and tragic stuff happens.

Parenthetically, in a subsequent career move I served as a consultant to a worker's safety and compensation board. In doing such work I reviewed quite a few files of current or former correctional officers whose applications for compensation had been approved. Some of the compensation claims ensued from physical injuries that the guards had sustained while on the job, usually arising from an assault by an inmate.

Increasingly common, however, were claims of psychological trauma, most often induced by repeated exposure to abusive and sometimes highly disturbing incidents such as inmate suicides, accidental deaths, and assaultive behavior up to and including murder. The guards also were quite vulnerable to being verbally abused, as well as to situations in which they were spat upon or, a perennial favorite, having feces and/or other bodily products cast their way.

Although such incidents are rare, relative to the number of guard-inmate interactions, and true verbal abuse or threatening behavior by inmates must be distinguished from the testosterone-fuelled posturing of guys showing off in front of their peers by standing up to the guards, the overall prison environment can be cumulatively demoralizing.

I can't speak to the genuineness of all the claims for PTSD being made by the guards – after all, we do live in an age of victimhood in which it seems that just about everyone can lay claim to having been exposed to some sort of trauma – but I have no doubt that most of the claims were quite legitimate.

The sight of someone who has hung himself, or cut open his carotid artery, or been stabbed multiple times or beaten beyond recognition, is not something that most of us encounter in our workaday lives. Or want to encounter.

Helo Hank

And who knows, it might have been the trauma of prison life that had prompted Hank, fondly lingering in my mind as 'Helo Hank' ('helo' being military-speak for helicopter), to do his absolute best to abscond from his penal placement. Or, like so many of us these days, he could have been someone who had been triggered by an unsafe space, and was just seeking closure and trying to recover… So much trauma, so little healing.
Whatever the motivation for Hank's hightailing hijinks – which we'll get to in a moment – the back story is that when he was still an upstanding member of the community Hank was a higher-level operator in the business of illicit drug distribution. In fact, in his day Hank was something of a regional boss in his field.

At one point, circumstances (usually in the form of territorial infringement, egotism, and a never-ending need to prove one's worth as a fierce and fearsome leader) had inspired him to eliminate the head of a rival drug faction. He'd accomplished such elimination by pointing the business end of a handgun in his competitor's direction and pressing the trigger.

This action, although undoubtedly fiscally sensible and potentially emotionally satisfying at the time, had the effect of terminating

Hank's drug cartel career after he was identified and convicted as the perpetrator of the murder and sentenced to life imprisonment.

By the time I saw him, Hank was many years into his sentence and was becoming grizzled as he settled into his middle years. Nevertheless, he had already managed to gain early release by persuading one of his underworld colleagues to commandeer a helicopter and use it to pluck him from the grounds of the maximum-security prison in which Hank was frolicking at the time.

Reports of the day indicate that while swooping into the prison grounds in the helo, one of Hank's faithful associates had fired at the guards from the air, wounding one of them (maybe my comment about the safety of the guards on the walls wasn't entirely accurate after all), and then had proceeded to whisk away Hank and another accomplice to freedom.

They were reported to have then buzzed off to a small island in a nearby lake, where undoubtedly they'd toasted their newfound freedom and androgenic daredevilry. Unfortunately, their celebrations and liberty were short-lived, because they were re-captured only a few days later and Hank was returned to the slammer in a fashion that was far less daring – in the back of a van – than the one in which he'd left.

By the time I interviewed him, a half dozen years after his escape, Hank had somewhat miraculously managed to get himself moved from a maximum to a medium security facility. Unsurprisingly, he came across as quite a nice guy – affably smiling and readily chatting, he was the kind of fella with whom you wouldn't mind having a beer, shooting tequila (not guards or rivals) and smoking a joint (not the prison kind).

But, as with most of these types, he had a steely core to him, and despite his superficial pleasantry there was no doubt in my mind that Hank was capable not only of assuming a position of leadership, but a position of alpha dominance and criminal command. Moreover, having already dispatched a rival to that great crack house in the sky, he clearly possessed robust and indeed deadly conflict resolution skills.

Of course, like others in his situation, Hank had a personal stake in making nice with his psychological evaluator, armed as he was with the knowledge that his intrepid interviewer's report could have a major impact upon whether he would be considered eligible for parole, lower security or some other benefit. The more intelligent and sophisticated offenders tend to be motivated and capable when it comes to playing the part of the charming, reformed and/or misunderstood offender.

Frequently, a certain degree of psychopathy, with a liberal dose of superficial charm and manipulativeness, also was involved. Nice guys to know, when you can do something for them and you aren't frustrating or angering them, but perhaps not so amiable when you're thwarting or opposing them. Think Tony Soprano or Vito Corleone.

Hank wasn't suffering from any type of mental disorder and didn't come across as being under-controlled or particularly impulsive. Although demonstrably capable of violence, and someone who could respond aggressively when provoked or threatened, his aggressiveness was more likely to be of an expedient or instrumental nature (that is, as a means to an end) than a spontaneous or at least unprovoked reaction. In one sense, he was a strong-minded businessman whose business happened to be illegal – as were his methods for eliminating the competition.

He'd also matured by several years since the time he'd committed murder. Overall, I saw him as being at medium risk for future criminal violence and as being more likely than not to behave appropriately in a lower security setting, as long as he continued to exhibit stable institutional behavior.

It turns out that I wasn't the only person to have found Hank to be a pleasant and affable fellow. Apparently, he managed to charm the socks and stockings off the parole board members, because a few years after I saw him, and despite his previous escape and his violation of a variety of prison rules early in his sentence, he was granted parole.

I don't know what he's been up to since then, and the chances are good that all his actions haven't been entirely legitimate, but if I run into him, I'll be sure to say hello. And to smile and do my best to be my usual agreeable and superficially charming and sincere self. (What's that old saying about it taking one to know one?)

Heads Will Roll

Aerial view of a federal maximum-security prison like the one in which the author conducted numerous assessments

One wonderful day I received a call from the warden of the maximum-security prison. The willowy and winsome warden (for indeed the warden was a woman) asked me to interview and assess one of their inmates, Scott, and then provide administration with advice as to how best to proceed with his case. Since his teens, Scott had accrued a lengthy history of offenses, including the infliction of violence (Scott believing in gender equality) upon both men and women.

At the time he came to my attention, he was serving a sentence for manslaughter: apparently, a few years earlier a woman had gone missing and eventually her body, minus its head, had been found buried in a shallow grave. The skull never was located. Exemplifying the sometimes convoluted and mysterious judicial process, initially Scott had been charged with homicide in the first degree but had been convicted of second-degree murder. However, following an appeal and retrial, he'd pled guilty to manslaughter and had been sentenced accordingly.

As a result, by the time he was sentenced for manslaughter, he'd already served several years of his sentence. An appeal can be a great way to get a head start (no sick pun intended) on the release process.

Although the motive for the murder remained unclear, the police and other reports on file revealed that while Scott was huffing, puffing, and moving his victim's body, her head had become separated from the rest of the corpse. As best as could be established, the victim's head had just fallen right off. (Don't you just hate it when that happens, and always at the most inconvenient time?!)

It was theorized that the woman's body had been decomposing for a while, and what with vertebral decay and the weight of the skull, her cranium had cartwheeled off amidst the hustle and bustle of the clandestine cadaver conveyance. I suppose that most of us have had the experience of losing our heads under duress, but this one takes the cake.

So far Scott had served his current sentence – first for murder and now for manslaughter – without too much difficulty. In fact, as I outline below, his behavior had been sufficiently satisfactory to enable him to apply for a family (aka conjugal) visit.

The problem being that prior to moving forward with sanctioning such a privilege, a psychological evaluation had been deemed necessary because Scott had adorned his cell wall with a photograph of a naked woman. Nothing wrong with a little libidinous decoration, the more liberal-minded among us may say.

The problem being that in Scott's case the woman in the photo was missing her head, the top portion of the photograph having been cropped from the image. Not surprisingly, such photoshopping (before there was such a thing) had caused a bit of a kerfuffle among the prison authorities, concerned as they were that Scott might be indulging in some sort of fetishistic fantasy related to decapitated naked females. After all, Scott had a bit of a history when it came to homicide and headless hijinks.

Compounding such concerns was the fact that given his appeal and re-sentencing for manslaughter, Scott had become eligible for personal family visits. Although such visits sometimes do include children, in Scott's case the plan was for him and his gal to play a game of hide-the-sausage in the private but secure accommodations situated on the prison grounds for just such a purpose.

Goodbye to the days of breaking rocks in the hot sun; hello to the days of breaking your balls in an air-conditioned trailer. Not exactly what most people have in mind when they talk about doing hard time, but there you have it.

You may well be asking yourself why a woman would be faintly, fleetingly or even forlornly interested in having a relationship with a gentleman with Scott's history. Well, it isn't unusual for a certain kind of woman to be attracted to a certain kind of fellow, including convicted felons such as murderers – even (especially?) those who have committed sexually motivated murder.

Some females find the darkness, sexuality, and power dynamics associated with male murderers and other violent offenders to be intriguing and, dare we say, sensuous. Sometimes, the darker the deed, the stronger the attraction: witness for example the mostly female participants in the Jeffrey Dahmer guided tours. And over time, communication between the admirer and the admired can blossom into a relationship. Every rock finds a crevice in which to roll.

On account of these circumstances, there was an understandable degree of consternation among prison management regarding the fact that if indeed Scott had been indulging in homicidal, offense-related fantasies with his headless nude model, it was conceivable that his female visitor and hider of sausage could be in danger of losing her head (literally – I assume that she'd already fallen for Scott in an emotional way) or otherwise being mistreated during a private visit.

I suppose that screaming headlines such as "Woman Gives Head During Prison Visit!" are the nightmarish scenarios that keep wardens and other government bureaucrats wakeful in the wee hours of the morning.

Unaccustomed as I was to be delving too deeply into the sexual connotations and connections between headless corpses, headless porn models and a headstrong prison visitor, with Scott's consent I forged ahead and formally assessed him. After doing that, I provided a written opinion to the prison authorities.

My evaluation of Scott followed the standard procedure of reviewing his clinical and correctional files, paying particular attention to the police reports, modus operandi, and witness and offender statements.

Next, I perused previous psychological assessment reports – which in this case offered no specific indication that Scott harbored any sort of paraphilia regarding decapitated damsels. Third, I interviewed Scott and gave him a few psychological tests.

What sort of tests did I give? Well, typically, psychological testing in forensic, as well as in more generalized assessments, consists of administration of: a) a fairly lengthy inventory of questions, the results of which provide information regarding the presence or absence of a mental and/or personality disorder and other behavioural and psychological tendencies and conditions; b) a test of intelligence or cognitive functioning; and c) as needed – depending on the reason for referral and the existence of any special factors such as suspected cognitive impairment or sexual problems – more specialized measures such as checks for malingering (faking illness), risk of re-offense/violence/sexual aggression, and tests or scales for anger and psychopathy.

The major differences between the first category of tests and some of the others – as well as many of the so-called psychological tests that can be found online and in various popular publications – is that the former tests are protected and restricted for use only by professionally trained and qualified clinicians.

They have also been the subject of considerable research, and they incorporate built-in validity scales with which to identify whether the person taking the test is trying to fake it in some way. Additionally, they have quite sophisticated sub-scales that are designed to identify whether the person is likely to be faking bad (pretending to be worse than they really are), faking good (pretending to be better than they really are), and the like. Given the high-stakes and adversarial nature of assessments conducted in connection with the criminal justice system, such validity checks are particularly valuable in a forensic context.

Faking bad, for example, tends to be of great concern in the forensic field, as well as in some civil litigation cases. Take the murderer who wants to feign mental illness to avoid a life-or-death sentence, or the accident victim who wants to appear more seriously incapacitated and pained than they really are.

Faking good also can be an issue in forensic evaluations, but such distortion tends to be more problematic in areas such as candidate selection/pre-hire evaluations – in which, for example, the law enforcement or pilot candidate is motivated to come across as being psychologically stable and pure of heart.

In contrast, many of the lower quality 'tests' are so easy to fake, intentionally or accidentally, that often they are little more than indicative or suggestive: they would require validated follow-up testing and/or clinical interview to confirm or disconfirm any information they provide.

An example of this might be a popular test inventory that furnishes information about how angry the person is and how that individual tends to express anger: the respondent checks off how he or she usually feels or behaves in various anger-related situations. There are no safeguards against distortion on this measure, and it would be easy for the person to tick the boxes which indicate that they control their anger and are as meek as mice, for instance, when in reality they're inclined blow up and break furniture and bones without much provocation.

The same is true for a couple of extremely popular measures of anxiety and depression. The 'pop' personality tests that are available online and elsewhere are even worse when it comes to potential fakery, quackery, and thus validity and value.

For obvious reasons, it can be downright dangerous to rely exclusively or even primarily on such transparent measures in high-stakes assessments in which liberty – and in civil cases very large amounts of money – are on the line. In such instances, you would always want to use as a basis for your opinion at least one of the major, authenticated tests that possess internal validity scales.

Incidentally, considering the sophistication and complexity of such measures, and the large amounts of diverse information they can generate, these days interpretation of the major tests is heavily reliant on computerized analysis, with the generated clinical hypotheses being subject to confirmation/disconfirmation, and if necessary modification, by the clinician who is responsible for reporting (and defending) the results and conclusions.

But back to Scott, the head guy: After undertaking all of the above steps I prepared my report on him, in which I combined the information I'd garnered from the various components of the assessment, and formed an opinion on the basis of which I made a recommendation.

I dutifully submitted my report to the prison management in which I said, in a nutshell, that although Scott clearly could be rather a mean-spirited, vicious, abusive, and homicidal hombre (hey, nobody's perfect and his girlfriend liked him), there was nothing to suggest that he was specifically attracted to decapitated dames. (Hey, they pay me to produce this stuff?)

Although I wouldn't have recommended that he receive private visits from anyone, and his record certainly conveyed that he could behave in a highly and repeatedly abusive manner toward women, there was no clear nexus between the headless pin-up and the index offense for which he was penned-up.

On a balance of probabilities (as we are wont to say in clinical reports when we can't say for sure but wish to communicate uncertainty while trying to sound learned and scientific), the pornographic photograph in question probably had no head because Scott was interested in the model's body, rather than her face – it may have been removed accidentally or perhaps deliberately detached as a means of objectifying the model and focusing on her female anatomical parts rather than her as human being.

Of course, I had absolutely no way to be sure of this, but as I said I was able to establish no obvious or compelling connection between the headless porn and the headless corpse, other than that they were both females. The available information suggested that the corpse's decapitation had been an unintentional rather than intentional consequence of Scott's predatory and perverse ways. There was therefore insufficient ammunition, from the headless factor alone, for me to formally propose a curtailment of Scott's private visits with his heedless lady friend.

On the other hand, if I were to have been asked, I would have strongly recommended against any woman forming a close relationship with Scott: he could be an ornery and mean-spirited fellow, including or perhaps especially when it came to his liaisons with the ladies, and sooner or later things tended not to end well for Scott's sweethearts. But there is no accounting for taste.

I heard nothing further about Scott regarding the visitation issue, which is a good thing, suggesting as it does that his amorous visitor kept her head and that Scott's sentence went ahead without significant difficulty. For the reasons outlined above, a couple of years later, having served most of his sentence, he was released from prison.

Alas, Scott simply could not bring himself to behave around the ladies, and a few years after that he reverted to type by holding a woman against her will for several days and punching her a few times while doing so. But credit where credit is due: he did allow her to keep her (bruised) head and – possibly because he was interrupted by the intervention of the police – her life.

I'm guessing that, despite his misogynistic misbehavior and penchant for pugnacity, Scott held some sort of macho magnetism or allure that was attractive to some women. Although he didn't favorably impress me, beauty very much is in the eye of the beholder. And even I, the red-blooded heterosexual male that I may have pretended to be, couldn't resist Scott's lure: a few years later a subpoena with his name and mine on it wended its weary way to my office, thereby commanding my presence in court to testify as an expert witness at Scott's dangerous offender hearing.

It seems that his record of violence, particularly toward women, finally had caught up with him, and the prosecution services were turning the tables and going after his head. And he was in danger of heading back to prison for a long, long time.

Although I always try – or at the very least try to appear – to be objective when giving my testimony, it's likely that my ensuing oral evidence in court helped the prosecution, because Scott's background and psychological profile suggested an antisocial personality disorder, generalized aggressiveness, power and control needs, hostility toward women, and a verified capacity to inflict very serious violence upon others.

At the end of the day (well, days – these hearings and trials can be long-winded affairs), Scott was declared a dangerous offender and was awarded the first prize of an indeterminate sentence – meaning that he would remain incarcerated until a parole board deemed him safe to be returned to society.

Given his age (around forty at the time), and the likelihood that he wouldn't be considered sufficiently harmless to be released until he'd 'burned out' by growing old, I'm guessing that Scott would be looking at around 20 or more years with which to admire the pin-ups, with or without their heads, on his cell wall.

A Brief Sexual Interlude

Although sadistic, homicidal and decapitation predilections were definite possibilities with Scott, there was nothing specific in his background to indicate that he derived sexual gratification from killing and beheading or mutilating women. However, some of the guys I have seen did enjoy such pastimes.

This pleasure seemed to have been confined at least predominantly to their sexual arousal and gratification, accompanying the devious delight they derived from dominating, overpowering, and sometimes humiliating their victims.

After the party was over, when no longer driven by their lust frenzy, some of these offenders seemed to experience at least rudimentary feelings of compunction about what they'd done – which would very much fall into the 'too little, too late' category of remorse but baby steps are better than no steps at all.

Of course, by the time I caught up with them, such feelings of regret had been intensified by the fact that they'd been apprehended, were in the process of being punished for their crimes, and often had participated in various rehabilitative or remedial programs that undoubtedly had taught them how best to convey, if not actually experience, their remorse.

Their expressions of regret most certainly provided no guarantee or even reasonable reassurance that they would not re-offend in a similar fashion, were they to be released – at least not without having undergone some sort of epiphany or other meaningful change or having developed a sufficiently severe aversion to getting caught and punished again.

As I've mentioned before, it's an unfortunate fact that, at least when it comes to the more serious sexual offender, it's often the case that such change very much involves the aging process. In most people the risk of sexual (and often other kinds of) re-offending decreases as the individual's age increases – crime generally being a young man's game. It may come as no surprise that the riskiest kind of adult male sex offender is likely to be young, with guys in the 18 to 25-year-old category being at the highest risk.

Another risky group is males who've committed offenses against children (the incest offender, who is the lowest risk sexual offender, being the exception) and/or those who have a paraphilia or sexual deviation that's been implicated in their offending.

So, the young child molester who is a pedophile (that is, preferentially sexually attracted to children) and the younger rapist who enjoys subjugating and violating females, would be quite high in terms of risk for sexual recidivism. At statistically highest risk for recidivism is the young guy who has offended against a male child.

Speaking of child molesters, it's important that we keep in mind a distinction that's usually glossed over or completely misunderstood by the media and a lot of others: many of those who offend sexually against children are not truly pedophiles, in the sense that their primary sexual preference is not for the slim, undeveloped body of the pre-pubescent child.

Although it's quite common for a guy who for example has sexually touched his granddaughter to be labelled a "pedophile", he'd be unlikely to fall into that relatively small percentage of individuals who prefers a child's body over an adult's, and as such it wouldn't be technically accurate to diagnose him as a pedophile.

As noted above, the incest type of offender, such as grandpa engaging in the regressive and substitutive behavior of fondling his granddaughter while bouncing her on his knee, is the type of sexual offender who is at the lowest risk for re-offense. Also, despite the loose use of the term in the media and elsewhere, the guy who sexually offends against a female teenager who has developed secondary sexual characteristics (breasts, rounded hips and buttocks) would likely not be a pedophile – just someone who is exploitative and/or immature and has very poor judgment and boundaries. (As an aside, these days some female teachers are getting themselves into hot water with their teenaged male students – usually, these women would be sexual offenders but not true pedophiles.)

Unless the person under examination acknowledges a deviant sexual preference, or their pattern of offending provides clear evidence of such a deviant sexual proclivity, reliably determining sexual interest is not a straightforward task.

An example of a clear-cut case of deviance would be a middle-aged guy who has never had an adult sexual partner, has committed sexual offenses against children, and belongs to an organization which promotes sexual interaction between adults and children. For instance, membership in a pedophile group such as NAMBLA (North American Man-Boy Love Association) usually is a pretty reliable marker of a sexual interest in children – although such information may be difficult to access within the context of your average forensic psychodiagnostic assessment, especially one being undertaken for the court, wherein the offender may well be defensive and even adversarial.

There are a number of sexual interest tests on the market, and each tends to have its own strengths and weaknesses. A principal problem to be overcome with all sexual interest tests, as with most medical tests, is that they can generate false positives and false negatives. A false positive on a sexual interest test would be it signalling sexual deviance when there is none; whereas a false negative would be the test showing no sexual deviance when such deviance exists.

The traditional, old-school method of testing sexual interest uses the penile plethysmograph (PPG), which is a device which, by using something known as a strain gauge, measures the degree of tumescence or swelling of the penis – which in turn tends to be a reliable indicator of sexual arousal in the male.

Typically, the client (for obvious reasons a biological male, although some research has been undertaken to measure changes in tumescence in the vagina) sits with the gauge wired around his willy while he looks at deviant and non-deviant sexually provocative photographs or listens to recordings in which various sexual scenarios are presented.

One of the principal problems with the PPG is 'flatliners,' who are those who don't respond at all to any of the stimuli: not entirely surprising, you may say, given the overall dynamics of the situation. (Mood music, candles, and wine usually being absent from the testing room.) Another problem with the PPG pertains to those who respond too much to everything, making it difficult to identify and score significant differences between various categories of sexual material.

A third problem with the PPG relates to the intrusive nature of the test, with both clinician and subject often feeling a touch uncomfortable during the procedure. All of which has led to legal challenges against its use and its discontinuation by some agencies.

In recent decades, visual reaction or visual response time has become a popular means of measuring sexual interest. For a few decades in my own clinical practice, I employed a sexual interest test that measures, very accurately, how long a person looks at the various images that are shown to him or her.

There are a couple of such tests currently available on the testing market. As with the PPG, these measures aren't perfect and they have their own shortcomings, but they're more user-friendly ("look mommy, no wires!"), and have received a fair amount of clinical and judicial acceptance.

In any case, sorting out who's interested in what is important when we're dealing with individuals who have offended in a sexually violent manner, especially if the sexual violence was directed against a child.

We want to know whether the person who perpetrated the offense is attracted preferentially to children, and therefore more likely to commit a similar offense in the future, or whether the action was a consequence of some other dynamic, such as opportunity, immaturity, and/or the unavailability of appropriate sexual outlets.

The fact that, for example, in our modern discourse and jurisprudence both a 15-year-old girl and a 5-year-old boy would be considered to be a child, has made it all the more important to determine whether an offender truly and primarily finds the younger body attractive, or whether his or her offense was for example of a substitutive nature.

The Horse Lover

Regardless of whether they have been assessed for sexual preference – and most have not – I've had the dubious honor of interviewing a multitude of sex offenders, many of whom had victimized children.

One guy, Phillip, stands out in my mind not so much because of the offense (which had involved the sexual molestation of a child) for which he had served time and a period of probation as it was for the reasons I discuss below.

My contact with Phil was a bit different from my normal routine because I got to see him on several occasions while he was in custody, as well as for a case management/risk assessment while he was on probation.

At some point early on during our encounters, Phil disclosed to me that he had the hots for horses. Equine amour. Now, there are some people who enjoy watching and even placing a small wager on the gee gees, and there are those who take delight in dressing and prancing as ponies – there are even gatherings for such aficionados of the trotting sports (check them out online if you don't believe me), which appear to be primarily linked to sadomasochistic and associated leather and latex themes, with an overlay of the horsey thing as something of a side dish.

But Phil was a purist when it came to his passion for the ponies: someone who very much enjoyed, quite literally, delving into horses' hindquarters.

And what's not to like? Being a well-read and broad-minded bibliophile, the reader may be familiar with Dr. David Reuben's 1960s classic tome "Everything You Always Wanted to Know About Sex" (subsequently satirized in a Woody Allen movie). If so, you'll know that for the average libidinous heterosexual human male, the rear end of a horse is rather a sensuous thing. Such sexiness, according to the good doctor, flows from the fact that when viewed from behind the steed's sleek curves and sashay are reminiscent of the adult female human's curves and sway, thereby rendering the horse attractive (at least upon some murkily semi-conscious level) to the healthy male.

I'm merely citing Dr. Reuben here, not necessarily endorsing his hypothesis – although it must be conceded that to some people those horsey hips are indeed something to behold. (And here's another Maddox Manson original: What do you call a boy horse who likes to dress up like a girl horse? Answer: A cross dressage!)

In Phil's eyes, equine erotica

But I fear that, as it's easy to do, I've wandered into a bit of an aside about horses' backsides. The point I was trying to make about Phil was that he liked horses. He liked them a lot. Indeed, his attraction to horses extended way beyond a vague affinity for the beast's mane, curvature and bearing, since his sexual interest in horses was both strong and compelling.

During our conversations, he indicated that he'd had a variety of pleasurable equine encounters and had found horses to be both intelligent and pleasing sexual partners.

In contrast, Phil coyly conceded, he had contemplated coitus with cows but had perceived in the eyes of the cows a certain lack of intelligence, and such unintelligence had squelched any budding bovine amour. It has oft been said that our principal sexual organ is our brain, and clearly Phil's brain was trotting him toward a specific form of inter-species sexual dalliance.

The problem being that Phil was a diminutive fellow, and in hindsight I couldn't help but ponder, from a practical perspective, exactly how he'd managed to hook up with a horse. I thought that perhaps a stepladder or a system of pulleys might have come in handy. Also, I couldn't help but wonder whether Phil ever had contemplated or enquired whether the horses had enjoyed his sexual overtures as much as he had.

Unfortunately, I never had the opportunity to chat with Phil about such intriguing possibilities and technicalities. Despite his equine attraction, Phil had gotten into trouble by offending against children, which signified that his sexual interests and activities made him a risk to society as well as to the stable, and that it would be best for my attention to remain focused primarily on his sexual offending against humans.

For the thing about Phil was that he was a sexual generalist rather than a specialist. Indeed, the last time I set eyes upon him we were at a dangerous offender hearing to which I'd been called to provide expert testimony. Wee Phil had reoffended against a child and at one point he'd blithely confided to his probation officer that he'd been entertaining homicidal fantasies regarding children.

Horses, homicide, and human children – an eclectic mixture. If I learned a lesson in this case, it was that even though Phil was a short, puckish, and potentially endearing guy with a self-disclosed appetite for ponies, he also posed a serious threat to humans – especially underage humans.

I testified to that effect, and Phil ended up being designated a dangerous offender and given an indeterminate sentence. From a clinical perspective there was nothing wrong with him mentally, other than having a generous helping of immaturity and a range of sexually deviant propensities. But clearly, Phil had demonstrated the capacity to act on his illicit fantasies and as exemplified by his offenses against children and horses, to go to some lengths to victimize others to meet his deviant sexual needs.

Phil's homicidal fantasies regarding children could not be discounted as mere passing whimsy, and this fact was reflected in the court's decision that he was indeed dangerous. A good call, I think, protective of both humans and horses.

Rick the Rapist

Rick was a ruffian and a rogue of a rapist. His claim to fame – the newspapers covered the story for weeks – was that he'd forced his way into a woman's home, brandished a knife, and devoted the next five hours of his life to torturing, repeatedly raping, and otherwise abusing his unfortunate victim.

But one of the unique features about Rick was that I had the opportunity to assess him twice – once as an adolescent when he was about to leave state care, and again as a young adult when he'd just been convicted of break and enter, unlawful confinement, and sexual assault with a weapon.

So, unlike a vast majority of the people I've dealt with, fate offered me the chance to delve carefully into Rick's background, see where he was at when he was 17 years old, and then take a look at how he was doing about 4 years later – by which time he'd progressed to being a convicted rapist and sodomizing sadist. A panoramic perspective and rarity for someone in the forensic psychology business.

Rick's story, which I present in relative detail in the following pages, provides some insight into the making of a monster. And while we peruse this account, I again ponder whether, had I been born into Rick's body and had experienced what he'd experienced, what magical ingredient would have made me turn out differently from him? Good intentions? Karma? A sunny soul? Star alignment? I don't necessarily have an answer to this question, but I simply offer it for consideration, in the spirit of "judge not, lest ye be judged."

When I saw him back when he was a teenager, Rick the Younger already had quite a history. His mother had left his family a few years after his birth, and not much later she'd perished from complications related to drug and alcohol abuse. Rick's father had physically abused him from an early age, and shortly after his mother left, his dad had taken off, leaving the young boy in the care of his extended family.

The members of his extended family also hadn't graduated *cum laude* from the Acme College of Good Parenting, and their home proved to be another unwholesome hole for Rick, in which he was subjected to neglect, further physical abuse, and sexual abuse. And while he was living with those relatives, their frequent moves had caused Rick to be repeatedly taken into temporary government care. A few years later, home conditions became so bad that the state gave up and transferred him to permanent foster care.

It may come as no surprise to hear that by the time he was taken into foster care, Rick was not the best-behaved boy on the block. He was prone to severe temper tantrums, stealing from people such as his teachers, aggressing towards younger kids, engaging in sexually inappropriate behavior, and being cruel to animals. The red flags (childhood animal abuse always being a great big one) were flapping wildly in the wind.

Although he was said to have made "excellent progress" in a therapeutic foster placement, his tenure in that home ended abruptly after he was found spying voyeuristically on his foster mother. He was moved to other so-called therapeutic residential placements, where he received some assessment and counseling, but by his early teens he was setting fires and behaving in sexually aggressive ways toward female adolescents.

Rick's problematic behavior continued unabated, with subsequent difficulties related to his offering of sexual favors to male peers and his spying on females: clearly, he was diverse in his distractions and his sexual interests. Indeed, not long after that he got into trouble for touching a pre-pubescent girl on the buttocks.

A little later, now in mid-teens, Rick threatened the staff and other residents at his group home, where he showed a propensity to behave aggressively and to wander casually into other residents' bedrooms. His behavioral difficulties, which were formally diagnosed as a conduct disorder, were further demonstrated by his escalating resistance to direction from residential home staff and his overall creation of a negative environment around him. His increased acting-out and aggressiveness, alongside a recognition that he was at risk for further sexual misconduct, finally resulted in him being placed in a secure treatment setting.

At this point we might ask what the heck was going on in the mind of a youth who was displaying such immensely unruly behavior? Some of the reports from the time hint at what might be expected to have been bouncing around in the brain of a boy who'd never known parental affection and who, from the very beginning of his life, had been subjected to a blend of rejection, abandonment, neglect, and trauma that had included physical and sexual abuse.

Who can blame Rick for reporting feelings of loneliness and depression? His sexualized acting-out, although certainly more blameworthy and illicit, was a byproduct of his own early abuse, precocious sexualization, and seething negative emotions.

And as a testament to the fact that there is little that can be done to effectively modify the thinking and behavior of those who show a very early-onset conduct disorder, throughout most of his childhood and for part of his adolescence Rick was seen by a variety of psychiatrists. He was, like many before and after him, started out on Ritalin to try to control his behavioral over-exuberance: some might say addressing the symptoms rather than the cause, which of course is much easier to do.

Later, Rick was prescribed a variety of medications, including antidepressants, in increasingly desperate attempts to get him to settle down. According to him, although he was seen by several mental health clinicians, he never really told them anything of importance, because he disliked talking about his problems.

His early rejection and other negative experiences had generated a self-protective and angry distrust of adults and authority figures such as pontificating psychiatrists and psychologists.

Despite all the efforts to get him to change his ways, by mid-adolescence Rick had begun to break into residences to increase his net worth. Over the next couple of years, he accumulated several criminal convictions for property offenses, as well as one for assault. In his group home he continued to display aggressive and other forms of problematic behavior.

His belligerence and offending behavior resulted in periodic stays at the local young offenders' facility, where he assumed something of a leadership role that was engendered in part by his displays of intimidation and aggression toward his fellow residents. He also got himself excused from group therapy by acting out whenever he was required to attend such groups.

When I first saw Rick, he was seventeen, living in a room and board situation, and neither working nor attending school. Although he claimed that he found academia to be easy, he had not been to school for about a year because well, he just didn't feel like it.

He was still in government care and devoting much of his time to hanging around the local downtown area with his friends. And although he wouldn't be high on my list of prom night dates, evidently he did possess a certain charm, reportedly having several "girlfriends."

As we chatted, I got the definite impression that Rick was glossing-over many of the details about himself and just going through the motions. And who could blame him? For most of his life he'd been psychologically poked and prodded by a motley assortment of mental health and social work professionals and undoubtedly (and wisely) he'd become very wary of, and well-defended around, those of that ilk.

Despite this, he was candid in his psychological tests, which suggested that at least superficially he was satisfied with himself – in fact inclined to come across in an arrogant and cynical fashion – and that he viewed the world in terms of power and control: to control or be controlled, to be powerful or to be powerless. Not altogether uncommon in people with Rick's history – or at least those who end up being seen by forensic psychologists.

Dominance and manipulation were the name of the game for Rick. Testing also indicated that consciously or unconsciously Rick tended to deny any problematic thoughts, feelings, and impulses. Further, and consistent with his record, the results signified that he was indifferent to social customs and rules. (Had the testing shown anything else, I would have thought the results to be wildly inaccurate.) Intelligence testing revealed that Rick was of about average intelligence, which was consistent with my clinical impression.

So, Rick at seventeen was exactly what you might expect him to have been, given his history. He had been abused and abandoned, and had come to bury his feelings, distrust the world and its so-called authorities, rebuff attempts to help him, and view his interactions from the perspective of vanquish or be vanquished.

He had also learned that physical aggressiveness helped him to survive and attain what he desired; in fact, such forcefulness came easily to a young guy whose life experiences had left him angry and conflicted. And oh yes, Rick was sexually promiscuous – a generalist rather than a specialist when it came to his sexual partner's gender, albeit outwardly displaying a preference for females. He also was sexually intrusive and potentially violent.

In my first report on Rick, which had been requested by the social workers and probation officers who were involved with him, I noted that when he wished to do so, Rick could come across as a likeable and presentable young guy. Unfortunately, and not surprisingly, the events of his past had affected him very negatively, instilling in him heightened levels of hostility and distrust.

I opined that although he'd never actually been charged with a sexual offense, he was at high risk for such a misdeed, as well as for more generalized forms of antisocial behavior. I made a total of nine recommendations, ranging from his not being in unsupervised interaction with children to his participation in the regional high-risk youth treatment program.

In the hope of getting him to settle down and feel better about himself – and reducing his penchant for breaking into homes – I also recommended that attention be paid to preparing him for some kind of suitable employment that might be of interest to him.

As reported in the press, about five years later the judge at his sexual assault trial questioned whether any of my recommendations had been followed. Apparently, no one was able to say whether they had been.

As a consultant from outside the geographical area (a local senior prosecutor once had laughingly shared with me his definition of an expert witness as being "some son of a bitch from out of town"), I hadn't seen Rick since my first encounter with him, and essentially my job had consisted of flying in, applying myself to a sometimes-gruelling schedule of evaluations and meetings, flying out, and then writing my reports.

So, before seeing Rick again – this time for a pre-sentence assessment – I had to rely completely on the information that was available on file to get a sense of what he'd been up to with his life.

Truth be told, having assessed at least many hundreds of guys and gals since I'd last seen Rick, and having an uncanny ability to forget about most of the people I saw (I prefer to think of it as a survival technique/defense mechanism, not as any failure of memory or lack of interest in the individuals I'd seen), I had no real memory of him. Fortunately, that made me simpatico with Rick, because it was obvious that he had no memory of having previously met me, either. Memorable to each other, evidently, we were not.

Now 21 years old, Rick's history since we'd last met was distressingly consistent with what might have been expected. For one thing, he'd begun to drink and take drugs in earnest and –

something he hadn't mentioned the first time I saw him – he tended to become even more aggressive when he consumed alcohol.

Although he'd experimented with various kinds of street drugs, he preferred alcohol, which had the unfortunate side-effects of further shortening his temper and periodically inducing alcohol-related blackouts.

At some point during our second conversation, Rick informed me that although his lawyer had told him that he should cooperate with the psychological evaluation, he could not stand psychologists. Obviously, our connection was beginning to bear the hallmarks of a mutual non-admiration society.

Undeterred by his burst of candor, I persevered with the interview and learned that, at least according to him and despite the nature of his offense, he'd had many sexual partners and even had lived with a young woman for a short period of time. The trouble was, I gained the definite impression that Rick simply couldn't be relied upon to tell the whole truth and nothing but the truth, especially when it came to bragging about his sexual prowess. Regardless, suffice it to say that according to Rick he was a lady's man who had been busy in bed.

As an aside, you may be asking why Rick seemed to have such an affinity for sex. Well, the short answer is that for many of us sex fulfills many needs, most of which are psychological in nature and in fact may have a lot less to do with teasing our tickle tackle than with our pacifying our brain boxes.

Recall that as a child Rick had been sexually abused. Also, he reported that as a young kid he'd been present while a couple had sexual intercourse, had watched sexually explicit movies as a child, and had his first coital experience while still pre-pubescent.

Given such precocious sexuality (even if not quite as described by him), it's probable that Rick learned very early on in life that sex could be a source of pleasure and distraction – a means of soothing away some of the negativity in his otherwise difficult and unstable childhood environment. It's also quite possible that he learned that sex was a way of currying favor from others, and a means of exerting power over them.

Certainly, for some highly sexually promiscuous people, sex is what is known as self-soothing behavior that takes away, or at least lessens for while, psychic pain. For a few, sexual activity can become highly addictive and self-destructive.

Whatever the underpinnings of his rampant sex life, and allowing for his propensity to tell porkies, it was reasonable to believe that by early adulthood Rick had danced with a fair number of partners and had lived with one or two young lasses. Despite such apparent availability of willing sexual connections, Rick had committed an offense during which he had broken into a woman's home, bound her with duct tape, blindfolded her, and repeatedly raped her vaginally and anally.

Rick had held a knife to her throat while making sawing motions, cut her, and over the course of the several hours that he and his victim had been together, had shown himself to be something less than a gentleman. The unfortunate woman eventually had made good her escape after Rick had fallen asleep – likely after the coke had worn off and the fatigue from his antics had set in. For her part, his poor victim may well have been in a state of fear-induced adrenalin arousal, which kept her alert and ultimately alive.

All of which begs the question of why would someone who had access to all kinds of consensual sex with women resort to such behavior? The answer is that Rick derived sexual and psychological gratification from the subjugation of his victim – controlling her, scaring her, hurting her, humiliating her and exerting complete domination and power over her.

The development of a misogynistic and fetishistic affinity for such ferocity has been the subject of earlier discussion, and likely revolved around Rick's early negative experiences with his mother (who'd abandoned him and eventually had committed the ultimate act of abandonment by dying while he was still a child – shades of Ken the Screwdriver, who had the castrating mother) and other unwholesome parental/adult figures in his life. Rick also had been sexualized prematurely and seemingly had become hypersexual. Mixed in with all of that was a whopping dose of generalized anger and aggressiveness.

Some of the psychological test results also hinted at another motivation for the dynamics of his offense: namely, an over-compensatory need to prove his masculine capability, and (I'm speculating a bit here) to perform with a level of sexual adequacy when he was raping someone that otherwise may well have eluded him.

During my interview of the Rick the Elder, he alternated between admitting his culpability for the offenses to which he had already pleaded guilty, denying that he'd committed them, and expressing his remorse for having perpetrated them. At first, he said that he had no memory for the events in question because he'd consumed liquor and crack cocaine for many hours prior to the offense.

He said that although he realized that what he'd done was wrong, he didn't know why he'd done it. Later in the interview, he asserted that such behavior wasn't at all like him, because he was a kind and generous person who treated the ladies well.

In the same interview Rick expressed his immense remorse for what he'd done, together with his dislike of how drugs and alcohol had changed him. Referring to his victim, he confirmed that neither of them had known each other prior to the offense, but conveyed his confidence that if she were to get to know him, she would see his "better half" and understand what a "kind, generous and big-hearted" (direct quotes) fellow he really was.

Rick genuinely believed this about himself, which I suppose says a whole lot about his way of thinking – or what in our line of work may be referred to as his cognitive distortions and faulty thinking. It's all in our perception.

Rick was covering his bases very well: according to him, he didn't remember committing the offenses, the offenses were out of character for him, but if he did do them, his behavior must have been due to his drug and alcohol use. These are always challenging defenses to work around when undertaking an assessment, so toward the end of the interview I hit him with the secret weapon that I'd been saving for best, which was the police report in which he'd admitted that he remembered his offense and his behavior during it.

Confronted by his statements to the police, he was finally obliged to acknowledge to me that in fact he did recall having committed the offending event. Laid bare in this way, he was unwilling to say anything more about his motivation and he became quite sullen and uncooperative – which was why I'd saved such a confrontation for the end of our encounter, when he'd already completed testing and most of the interview: if I was going to get under his skin and unleash his contrariness, first I wanted to ensure that I'd done everything else I needed to get done.

That's the thing about defensive, bragging and fibbing guys like Rick: a skilled forensic examiner needs to parse through the verbiage and tease out reality from wishful thinking, half-truths, and blatant lying. Some of the psychometric tests that we use can be helpful in determining the individual's overall level of cooperation and truthfulness, and as discussed previously some of the more comprehensive and sophisticated ones are good at doing so. But at the end of the day, it's up to the clinician to get a sense of the accuracy and veracity of the person's statements and assertions.

Clinical analysis was especially required in Rick's case, because the results of the personality test that was administered to him, which contained several internal validity checks, hadn't suggested that deception had undermined their accuracy.

However, testing had supported my clinical impression that Rick remained free from any kind of major mental or emotional disorder. At the same time, personality test subscales suggested that he was exhibiting borderline features (borderline as in borderline adjustment, meaning that significant psychological and emotional dysfunction was likely to be present, but not to a degree of a major mental disorder) and that he was inclined to have difficulty coping with life and enjoying good relationships with others. Interestingly, test interpretation also revealed Rick's feelings of tension, edginess, dependency, and inadequacy.

Intelligence testing again signified functioning within the average range and there was nothing wrong with his memory or overall cognitive functioning. He was, based on the criteria commonly used to establish such things, sane: he was in contact with what usually passes for objective or agreed-upon reality. Also, from a legal perspective he was aware that his offense was wrong, and that at the time he was committing it he knew it to be wrong.

It didn't come as a huge surprise that when rated for psychopathy, Rick scored quite high. Descriptors such as callousness, remorselessness, and selfishness tend to be appropriate for people like Rick. In addition, when I deployed some specialized risk scales (discussed in more detail in the following chapter) to rate Rick on his potential for violent and sexual recidivism, he was scored as being at considerable risk both for violent and sexual reoffending.

An aggressive, power-oriented, moderately psychopathic guy with sexual hang-ups and a substance-use problem, who had been rated as being at high risk for violent and sexual recidivism. What could possibly go wrong?

In my report to the court, I opined that Rick was dishonest, self-serving, and at least sometimes insincere. I communicated my impression that he was a troubled young man whose formative experiences had left him with a chaotic sense of himself and his world.

Rick hadn't shown any depth of genuine remorse for his victim, and in fact his capacity to experience true empathy and similar feelings was likely to be woefully lacking. Already at high risk for sexual and violent recidivism, his use of intoxicants would further increase the probability of his acting out impulsively and aggressively.

I went on to say that in a prison setting, Rick required a good dose of structured and intensive sex offender, substance abuse, and anger management programs. Potentially, he could also benefit from whatever educational and vocational training opportunities were available to him, but only time would tell whether he'd be willing to partake of such golden (and free to him) opportunities.

I also recommended that when he was eventually returned to the community, he should be provided with as much external supervision and structure as possible (translation: watch this guy – he's at ongoing high risk, no matter what treatment and other remedial programs he's taken while in custody, and no matter what claims of positive change he may make).

As I mentioned earlier, the reality is that although some programs do help to reduce recidivism for most people, for guys like Rick it is more likely that their risk will decline meaningfully only as they age and prove themselves capable of remaining offense-free in the community for several years.

I recall having testified to that effect at Rick's sentencing hearing, during which I was tasked with reiterating and defending the general findings of my report. As in all such situations the lawyer who had asked me to testify led me through my report, sometimes going line by line, in his attempt to underscore and elaborate on my findings.

Next, the defense attorney cross-examined me, subtly and not-so-subtly seeking to undermine my report and credibility, or at the very least to present the client in as positive a light as possible. ("So, when you say that my client is worse than 75% of other inmates, that means that he's better than 25%, correct?") Then, the first lawyer asked clarifying questions in re-direct examination. Finally, the judge had his turn asking questions – mercifully, he only had a couple, and unlike the defense questions they weren't designed to damage my credibility, trick me, or hurt my feelings.

According to the subsequent media reports, the judge had anguished over an appropriate sentence for a young fellow who had, as the judge saw it, been failed by the state that now wanted to punish him. I can't help but think about what was going through the mind of Rick's victim, as the judge pondered such issues and pontificated about society's failures.

Although I'm not a hang-them-high kind of guy, the dynamics of Rick's offenses, superimposed on his psychological make-up and his estimated level of risk, warranted a significant stretch in the joint, hopefully long enough to provide him with ample time to reflect, mellow, comprehend, and mature.

The judge gave Rick a sentence of a little under nine years, of which he ended up serving about six before he was released on parole. As a condition of his release, he was required to reside in a half-way house that was operated by the correctional authorities, with tight restrictions on his freedom of movement.

Unfortunately, Rick ended up going AWOL from the half-way house: not once, not twice, but thrice. He was re-captured and re-incarcerated each time, but subsequently released yet again to his half-way haven.

Such behavior didn't exactly speak to his having been rehabilitated and socialized by his penitentiary experiences. In fact, I would not have been at all surprised to learn that he'd become a more hardened and aggressive individual during the five or so years that he'd been incarcerated.

I don't know what happened to Rick after that or where he is today – which, to be perfectly honest, doesn't worry me, as long as he doesn't show up at my place. My guess would be that he would wander in the direction of more time in prison, homelessness, addiction, and likely a very premature death. I hope that I'm wrong and that he's miraculously reformed his ways and is doing okay. But most of all I hope that he hasn't created any more victims along the way.

There's always a mixture of emotions when I think about someone like Rick. On the one hand, he was an unfortunate creature who really didn't have much going for him from the very beginning of his life. One could, and indeed should, feel compassion and a degree of sympathy and empathy for such a life course.

On the other hand, Rick channeled the consequences of his formative experiences into a cauldron of boiling hostility that led him to inflict very serious pain on someone else. He had sadistically and irrevocably altered the course of his victim's life, and his offending behavior, sustained as it was over an extended period, was extremely cruel, and undoubtedly has left deep and permanent psychological scars on her.

So, although we may feel some pity and regret regarding the factors that created Rick, it can be difficult to hold onto those sympathetic feelings while contemplating the serious harm that he had inflicted upon an innocent person.

Chapter Three
The Riches of Risk

Over the choppy course of my career, a sea change has occurred in the way in which risk is assessed. Back in the good old days we'd relied primarily on the hoary, handed-down clinical principles that we'd been trained to believe were true. Then we applied those principles to the assessment at hand and arrived at our "clinical judgment" regarding the individual's risk level.

An example of this is one of the beliefs that we used to embrace as gospel – namely, that a sex offender who denies his offense is automatically at higher risk than the sex offender who admits his or her guilt: although this might appear to be quite intuitive and reasonable, it turns out that the universal application of this principle has not been found to be evidence-based.

During the past twenty to thirty years a great deal of professional journal real estate has been devoted to a discussion of evidence-based assessment and treatment. Although the very concept of "evidence-based" has been questioned, no one can really argue with the notion that any intervention or evaluation should be based upon facts derived from research, as opposed to, say, a whimsical hunch or a belief that the old way is the best way.

Coinciding with the recognition of the merits of evidence-based decision-making, in the 1980s researchers and marketers began to develop and (most importantly) sell tests with which to augment, and in some cases replace, subjective decision-making. Now, some clinicians – particularly those who are extremely fearful of being accused of making any kind of mistake in their clinical conclusions or having to substantiate their opinions and decisions without a superfluity of tests upon which to fall back – tend to use many, and sometimes too many, tests.

I've seen some psychological reports that would have made marvelous paper weights and door stops: if purveyed by the pound, their authors would have been wealthy. However, I've seriously wondered whether anyone has read those kinds of verbose reports all the way through, before unceremoniously skipping to the summary section. I know that I haven't.

Nevertheless, psychological testing has become big business. Excessively big business. There are tests for everything you could imagine, running the gamut from anger and autism to memory, mood, malingering, neurocognition, trauma and visuospatial functioning – with about every other conceivable aspect of human behavioral and psychological functioning now being the subject of some sort of marketable "standardized" test.

But what has really revolutionized forensic risk assessment has been the development of predictive scales and inventories with which to estimate the potential for future violence, sexual offending, and general criminality.

By using such risk predictive tools the assessor can establish, with varying degrees of accuracy and reliability, the likelihood that Mr. or Ms. X will engage in Behavior Y. Usually, but not always, such probability is expressed in nominal terms, typically low to high. However, with some scales, such as a widely used measure that's used to determine the long-term risk of sexual recidivism, the probability of re-offense can be communicated in different ways, up to and including an absolute or specific numeric probability over a specific number of years.

The caveat to such predictive magic being that just as life insurance actuarial scales can't be used to predict when a particular person will drop dead (they can only categorize your overall morbidity risk based on your age, gender, body mass index, and so on), it's impossible to predict if and when a particular person is going reoffend sexually: we can only say that the individual falls into a group of similar people who on average have Z probability of re-offending in Z years.

The allure of such risk assessment scales seems obvious. How terribly compelling and reassuring to be able to say, with an objective test to back up your opinion, which offenders are at higher risk and therefore need to have treatment and supervision resources prioritized for them – or to be locked up for a long time, sometimes indefinitely.

An additional incentive for using such scales, particularly in large bureaucratic agencies in which there is a pool of modestly paid front-line staff, is that sometimes line personnel can complete the risk scales, thereby circumventing the need to pay for an expensive professional opinion. Indeed, such was the logic which prevailed in a probation service with which I used to do business: why pay for costly psychologists, when we can have probation officers complete standardized, formulaic risk assessments?

(Although the research data suggest that such empirical risk assessments can furnish predictive information that's as accurate as that provided by a good clinician, anecdotal feedback from line staff signifies that the other kinds of information associated with a forensic psychological evaluation, such as discussion of specific risk mitigation and case management strategies, is sorely missed when the assessment is comprised solely of line staff completing a standardized form. And with the advent of Artificial Intelligence, we'll soon reach a point at which even the lower-paid line staff will be redundant when it comes to risk evaluation.)

So now forensic psychologists have some popular risk assessment tools which help them to determine the risk of re-offense for violent and sexual offenders. Essentially, what such measures do is list a number of factors which, if present in the individual being assessed, increase his or her risk. The factors in question usually are derived from what are called meta-analytical studies: studies of a whole bunch of studies, from which are identified the variables most likely to be associated with re-offense.

From that group, the most critical factors are listed in the risk assessment scales, alongside the procedure for scoring and interpreting the scale. Most of the tests are designed to make money for the test developers and marketers. A few – including a couple of the best and most highly-used ones – are provided without cost, essentially as a gift to the clinical community and by extension society as a whole.

A primary example of such a test is a current risk assessment measure for sex offenders, offered free of charge, called the Static-99R. The Static-99R consists of only ten items but has been found to be reasonably accurate (moderate levels of accuracy being the best that these tests currently can offer), and certainly better than the mere hunch or clinical judgment of most of today's mental health clinicians.

A measure such as the Static-99R not only enables the assessor to determine into which category of risk a particular individual should be placed – ranging from very low to well above average – but to predict the probability of sexual recidivism for someone in a given category over a certain period of time.

This ability, which as we've discussed is analogous to the actuarial tables employed by insurance companies, can be quite useful. Of course, it's also subject to misuse, especially if it's forgotten that a particular person's probability of re-offense can never really be known and in any case should be used as only one component of a more comprehensive risk assessment. Unless of course, you're artificially intelligent.

The Static-99R and its ilk have become very popular among those in the risk prediction trade. Not only have they been used in routine classification and decision-making on the front lines, but also in the high-stakes realms of, for instance, sexually violent predator (SVP) evaluations in various regions throughout the United States. SVP laws are those associated with the committal of dangerous sex offenders to state-run detention facilities following the completion of their prison term.

Given the serious ramifications of such detention, and the potential for misuse, there is a great deal on the line in such assessments. And despite the standardization of the assessment measures and their scoring criteria, it isn't unusual to see two rival experts in court – one hired by the defense and the other by the state – testifying and bickering about the correct scoring of the scale: potentially, a single point can make a big difference in the appraised risk level, and thus have a major impact upon whether the individual will continue to languish in custody.

A person's freedom being on the line, it's extremely important to ensure that the clinicians using the tests know what they're doing. Unfortunately, such competence is not always to be found, even in high-level and high-risk evaluations such as the SVP ones.

Measures such as the Static-99R are relatively sophisticated in terms of their scoring and their predictive capacity, but at the same time elegant in their simplicity: for example, it's usually a fairly straightforward matter to score how old the offender will be at the time he's released to the community (age being an important risk factor), as is the guy's offending history.

As noted, the Static-99R also is available without cost for use by trained clinicians and similar professionals. Other scales, however, advertise themselves as being able to help the clinician make a more "informed decision" and to enhance their "professional judgment" regarding the presence or absence of risk factors, and on that basis to estimate the person's risk level.

Regardless of the assertions of their creators, who for the most part make good money from selling such scales, a certain amount of subjectivity, and thus the potential for conscious or unconscious bias, can creep into their scoring.

But at the end of the day, it's fair to say that the use of such risk assessment aids has radically altered and improved the predictive accuracy of forensic psychological examinations.

I've used such measures in my own clinical decision-making – and have been challenged to explain the scoring procedure and defend my scoring methodology in court – and have found them to be useful. In the main, they've tended to support my own judgment as to risk and have been particularly useful in providing a rationale and a structure for the communication of my risk appraisals.

All that said, as with all such increasingly automated evaluations, there's an element of peril when discretion is removed from the decision-making process, and this is likely to be especially true for lesser-trained individuals working in the trenches of corrections.

My own experience has led me to believe that removing the human from the decision-making equation and relying totally or primarily on an assessment scale, test or computer program is not the most productive or most fair route to take. But additional research has indicated that with some measures (for example the Static-99R) predictive accuracy declines when the clinician tries to override the test results. And who am I to doubt such research?

Chapter Four
The Lucrative Small Change Business

I don't want to give the impression that I've only dealt with the likes of Rick and Phil, and that all of my professional life has been tied up with salacious sex offenders, bondage aficionados, and their balls-bothered brethren. I've also assessed salubrious citizens such as bank robbers, thieves, and "dine and dashers" (those who get their exercise by walking briskly out of restaurants after enjoying their meal without bothering to pay for it).

I've learned along the way that although we can intellectually understand and often predict the behavior of such people, usually (always?) we can't change them unless, as the trite but true old adage goes, they really, really want to change. And then again, the leopard's spots may fade a bit over time, but seldom do they disappear entirely. Some people just think differently, and many don't perceive a need to change.

They are either too dumb, egotistical, complacent, and/or contented with their high reward-low energy expenditure lifestyles to be ready for a career switch. And some people really do simply seem to have a part of their brains – the bit that serves as a moral compass – missing.

Sid the Kid

Take Sid.

A fair-haired guy in his early twenties, albeit emotionally quite a bit younger. When our paths crossed, Sid was a guest at a pre-trial detention center. Sid's modus operandi was to break into vehicles, which he did by the hundreds, and to help himself to whatever he could put into his plump and pasty hands. I can still recall him impishly and smugly smirking as he bragged to me about how he would cleverly punch a small hole just below the driver's side car door keyhole, thereby deactivating the electronic master lock and unlocking all of the doors.

Now, given that I'd recently shuffled out to my own car one fine morning only to discover that it had been broken into, and that a small hole had been drilled beneath the driver's side door lock, my interest was piqued by this discussion. I therefore spent some time chatting with Sid – a guy with whom I would ordinarily have spent just long enough to ensure that he was not crazy, suicidal, and/or homicidal.

And as I spoke with him, pique turned to peeve, and the urge to smack him a good one across the side of his big head may – and I only say may – have flickered momentarily across my subconscious mind.

What was fascinating about Sid was the fact that he displayed absolutely no capacity to reflect upon the immorality of his destructive and costly thievery, or to exhibit any ability to contemplate how he might have felt, had he been the victim rather than the victimizer. In general, such inabilities and lack of concern tend to be associated with intellectual limitations as well as with the trait of psychopathy, which was mentioned above.

In turn, psychopathy is highly likely to be the end-product of a blend of the individual's early formative experiences and some sort of biological predisposition to the development of psychopathic characteristics.

Although the relative causal contribution of biology and the environment remains unclear when it comes to psychopathy, it has clearly been the case that both a genetic predisposition and certain early experiences have been present in most of the psychopaths I've had the pleasure of meeting. It's entirely possible that childhood events – of a type which promoted the individual's emotional detachment from their actions as well as from their connection with and caring for other people – are associated with the development of structural changes in the brain.

It remains unclear whether the environmental experiences cause the physical changes, whether the brain somehow has to be different or altered in the first place in order for the environmental experiences to work their psychopathic magic, or whether there's some sort of as-yet mysterious interplay between the two, culminating in the development of psychopathy.

Or the physical changes may merely be a correlation of psychopathy, and not causal at all. We can have our opinions, but all we know for sure is that psychopathic traits are real and that when they're present to a significant degree, the affected individual tends to be attuned to the needs of no one but herself or himself and is inclined to see others more as objects than as living, breathing sentient beings worthy of any altruistic interest or attention.

The point being that, just as it's impossible to talk a person into having a conscience or even an ounce of genuine consideration for others when that individual lacks the motivation or apparent capacity for such change, it's generally a waste of time and energy to try to convince prolific and egocentric thieves or other exploiters that they should be experiencing feelings of compunction regarding their behavior. They simply are not able and/or willing to get it.

It's the equivalent of water trickling off a duck's back, and although some people may have (lovingly and jokingly, I'm sure) referred to me as a quack, I do value my time and sanity enough not to waste my limited intellectual resources on trying to talk people into changing what they don't want to or can't change.

It's important to keep in mind that people think differently and that just because Mrs. Manson may, in my wildest dreams, think of me as an intelligent, witty and all-round great guy who should be heeded at all times, in no way does that mean that others will pay any attention to anything that I have to say. Or try to change their world view so that it matches my view. For many of the people I have run across in my business, doing the right thing is a very relative and subjective concept, revolving around the concept that the right thing for them is based entirely on what benefits them, often over the short term.

Which brings me to a discussion about the treatment of sex offenders. As I indicated earlier, it used to be believed that if a sex offender could be persuaded to overcome his denial of his offense, to adopt the viewpoint of the victim, and to develop an altruistic awareness of the kinds of personal changes that would be required to lower his (or her – society is slowly coming to recognize that females can and indeed do commit sexual offences) risk of re-offending, he was on the road to risk reduction, redemption and rehabilitation.

For the most part, sex offender treatment still tends to revolve around such psycho-educational principles, which distilled to their essence entail getting the offenders to: a) see where and why they went wrong; b) understand the necessary cognitive and behavioral steps to undo such errors; c) recognize and avoid risk factors; d) realize why it's in their and everybody else's best interest not to repeat such errors; and e) go forth and sin no more.

The trouble is that the effectiveness of such treatment is highly dependent upon whether the offender genuinely wants to modify and control their behavior. It would be a safe bet to say that at least a few sexual and non-sexual offenders only want to implement the changes necessary to help them to avoid further legal trouble and if incarcerated to facilitate and expedite their release from custody.

However, focused as it must be upon what are practical and sometimes superficial changes, usually presented in a group format reinforced by independent study and reflection, treatment as it's presently conceived is unlikely to be particularly effective in generating substantive change in the sex offender's core beliefs and core self. Of course, that's not to say that such treatment is useless or that it should be discontinued, it's merely to note that in my experience it has been limited in terms of its depth and efficacy.

What is worse is the possibility, which has been uncovered by experience and research, that some individuals (especially those with elevated psychopathic traits) who undergo some types of so-called therapy derive absolutely no benefit from such participation.

There's even evidence that they can become worse sex offenders because of their involvement in rehabilitative sex offender treatment programs. These are the people who are adept at learning and parroting the jargon, and who can therefore talk the talk and act in ways that create a favorable impression, but who do not experience any sort of meaningful change in their beliefs, behavior, or risk of recidivism.

Making a Better Worse Sex Offender

Which reminds me of a guy I first saw back at the very beginning of my career when he was on probation for having sexually molested a child. Frank was an affable and smooth-talking fellow with nice wavy brown hair, brown twinkling eyes and a charming smile. He was punctual and regular in his attendance at the sex offender group treatment sessions – which in those days were held at a specialized supervision probation office – and his participation in the groups was incredibly good.

By all appearances, he was committed to reducing his risk and keeping his nose, and all other relevant body parts, clean. Despite his surface cooperation and keenness, Frank turned out to be a very risky, repeat sex offender. And although he dropped out of my professional life for about two decades, during the intervening years his sexual misdeeds persisted and resulted in his continuous involvement with the criminal justice system.

In fact, he finally re-entered my life as a high-risk sex offender who was being monitored by law enforcement and probation services in a coordinated police/probation supervision program in which I was involved as the psychological consultant.

Eventually, Frank had let it be known that he'd very much enjoyed the sex offender treatment groups and had gotten something out of them, thanks very much. Unfortunately, what Frank had mostly got out of the groups was sexual titillation and temptation. It turned out that he had got off on listening to others' accounts of their offenses, as well as from the overall sexual focus of the groups.

So much so, in fact, that after each group he'd partaken of healthful exercise by strolling through nearby neighborhoods, where he'd actively sought out voyeuristic and related sexual opportunities – shimmying up walls, peeping in windows, seeing what there was to be seen, and making himself available for any and all sex offending opportunities.

Alas, Frank's sex offender treatment had been a flop. In large part such floppiness was attributable to the fact that good old Frank was pretty darned psychopathic – a charmer who could slickly talk the talk and baffle the gab, but who was both deceitful and self-interested. As this is being written, Frank continues to be monitored as a high-risk offender, receiving enhanced supervision by police and probation.

I doubt very much that anyone has put his name on the list for participation in additional sex offender treatment. But hope springs eternally among many clinicians and program facilitators, budgets have to be used up, and empires have to be enlarged, so nothing really would surprise me.

Of course, some people do derive benefit from their involvement in sex offender and other forms of mandated programs, and statistics show that overall, sex offenders' risk of recidivism is reduced by their active participation in good quality, structured treatment programs. It's just that it would be naïve to believe that all or most offenders are automatically at reduced risk once they've participated in rehabilitation curricula, or that all or most offenders should be routinely referred for treatment.

As with all forms of therapy or counselling, the offender's motivation to better understand and comport themselves has to be genuine, and the treatment has to be evidence-based and pragmatic, for it to be helpful. Otherwise, it may do no good whatsoever – and sometimes it does bad.

Domestic Disharmony

Which, while we're discussing so-called treatment, brings me to my admittedly partisan and somewhat jaded opinions concerning the efforts that I've seen being put into domestic or intimate partner violence programs. During the 1990s, a strong focus was brought to bear on domestic assaults (which in those days meant male violence perpetrated against females), and any allegation of significant relationship disharmony or alleged domestic violence typically resulted in the automatic arrest of the involved guy.

In a large majority of cases, this had the effect of numerous men being convicted of assault, usually with the imposition of probation and sometimes a period of incarceration. As a condition of their probation, most of the domestic violence guys were ordered to attend and participate in intimate partner violence counselling programs.

I have interviewed hundreds of those guys, all of whom had been placed on probation for acts of reported aggression against their female partners. I've also read the related police reports and victim statements and listened to the guys' stories. In many of the cases it was apparent, and sometimes acknowledged by them, that they'd been unreasonably aggressive and that their behavior warranted sanction.

In other instances (and there was overlap – the course of true love never running smoothly), it was clear that the volatility was a symptom of a dysfunctional marital relationship in which both partners had been guilty of psychological and physical aggressiveness. Although when push came to shove (and there are exceptions), the guy's larger size and physical power often meant that he had inflicted greater damage upon his female partner than she had inflicted on him.

In some instances, it was reasonable to assume that the female in the relationship was using her own power to pick up the telephone as a weapon against her partner, and in effect she was employing the state (via the police) to punish her spouse. Many was the time I heard a refrain from a guy on probation that went something like: "She hits me as much as (or more than) I hit her, but I'm the one who's on probation. When we argue she blocks my way and stops me from leaving. She taunts me, telling me that she can call the cops. When I try to push past her to leave, she phones the police." Sometimes, after the couple had cooled down the female partner had regretted – or had been persuaded to regret – such behavior, and she had attempted to retract her complaint, but by then the legal machinery had ramped up into full operational mode and the guy's detention and new criminal charges were a foregone conclusion.

Self-preservation forbids me from becoming the sour cream in the political hot potato of whether females are as inclined as their male counterparts to resort to physical aggression in their relationships – although some high-quality research suggests this to be the case, and that it's only in the more extreme cases that males perpetrate the worst violence. I will merely note that the belief that only guys can be aggressive and only gals can be victims is, to be charitable, quite simplistic and/or gender political.

Even more unwise, in my estimation, was the way in which the correctional psycho-educational programs, which were run by the probation offices, were administered. Pared to the bone, these programs lectured and hectored the male probationers regarding the error of their ways, and the need for them to be respectful and peaceful in their relationships.

Although undoubtedly founded on noble principles, with the worthy aspiration of trying to protect women and make for a better and more harmonious society, assuming that the identified person (namely, the guy on probation) was the only problem in the relationship clearly was like trying to solve a jigsaw puzzle with only half of the pieces.

Like the guys who were beheaded during their hanging, the execution left something to be desired. Indeed, there was something disturbing and counterproductive about the mass implementation of these programs – particularly because the courses with which I was familiar were facilitated by female probation officers, many of whom were still in their twenties or early thirties.

Picture if you will a scenario in which there is a room full of men who have had problems in their relationships with women. Now imagine them being made to listen to a series of scripted classroom lectures, delivered by a couple of young women, about how they should be behaving better.

Pause this mental video for a moment and reverse the genders – visualize a room full of women who have had problems in their relationships with men, being lectured to by a couple of young guys about how they need to gain better control of their emotions and behave more nicely toward their partners. You can imagine how these programs were received by many of the male probation clients, and of how helpful they were to those guys and their relationships.

Also consider whether there was the possibility of what's known in the medical business as *iatrogenic effects*: when the intervention causes or worsens the illness. In this case, intensified resentment on the part of the offenders, who received the oft-repeated message that all of the blame was on their shoulders, and that the female probation officers were there to underscore in their minds just how bad they'd been and how much better they should be in their dealings with their womenfolk.

Well-intentioned, perhaps. Agenda-driven and satisfying to some people, possibly. Helpful – I don't know, but probably not in most cases.

Such programs still existed when I stopped consulting to the probation services about ten years ago. I'm not sure whether they continue to be presented in such a fashion, although I would suspect that, at a bare minimum, attempts have to be made to implement some semblance of gender balance in the program facilitators. (Heck, even a team of male and female presenters could model how two adults can get along as a harmonious team – what a novel idea!)

However, I do know that it slowly began to dawn on the authorities, and I believe the larger society, that men are not the only ones who can behave in dysfunctional ways in relationships, and that indeed women also can be physically as well as psychologically aggressive and abusive.

This increased awareness, as difficult as it was for some (especially well-funded women's groups) to acknowledge, resulted in the implementation of policy changes. So, although the police were still required to look at events through a "gender lens", men no longer were automatically arrested whenever there was a complaint of domestic assault or disharmony. Indeed, some women found themselves being arrested and charged with assault.

That said, there's no doubt that in general the biological human male is physically larger and stronger than the biological human female, and that although research indicates that the most common type of intimate partner violence is bilateral and reciprocal, with both the lad and the lady giving and taking with equal gusto, most of the cases of really serious violence, domestic or otherwise, are committed by guys.

I have been (professionally) involved in many cases of nasty, aggravated assault and its equivalent, and I can recall that although a majority of them involved men aggressing toward other men, there were a few in which the victims were women.

Blame the androgenic hormones, socialization, or a combination thereof, but once such blame has been attributed, what to do? If the violence is serious and habitual, confinement and the provision of longer-term treatment/rehabilitation programs, if appropriate for a given offender, may be of some help. But don't just lecture the guys and tell them to shape up, be gentler and more sensitive (i.e., more feminine), and do better.

And don't just offer a seriously violent person a little counseling and encouragement and hope that he'll go away and sin no more: that's the lazy and simplistic way out. Instead, in the case of domestic conflict, start by offering training to both of the involved parties on how better to manage their emotions and lower the likelihood of violence. Address the relationship issues that underlie the abusive behavior, whenever possible working with both partners: sometimes it's a dyadic and sometimes symbiotic problem, not simply one person being bad, and one person being victimized.

And do provide the physically abusive person with evidence-based psycho-educational training on how to communicate emotions and in particular anger and frustration in peaceful ways.

However, if one of the involved parties truly is unable to control his or her aggression, and the probability of continued violence appears to be high despite any 'counseling' types of intervention, then the consequences for truly repetitive forms of aggression – and again, I'm not talking about mutual, relatively low-level violence, with the guy doing more damage than the woman simply because he's bigger – then external sanction for the offending partner needs to be appropriately severe. And by severe, I mean serious jail time and where possible enduring court-ordered, reciprocal, and enforced restraining orders.

On the subject of counseling, to close off this undeniably controversial discussion about treatment, and at the risk of incurring the wrath of many of my professional colleagues, I have to admit that I'm not a big fan of a lot of the so-called treatment and counseling being offered by some of today's mental health clinicians. It's very expensive (upwards of $250 per 50-minute therapy hour at the time of writing) and for many an unattainable form of intervention and assistance that doesn't necessarily live up to its hype: in fact, it can be quite marginal in terms of being of lasting assistance.

Sometimes – as in the case of poorly qualified or completely unqualified 'counselors' who have not begun to resolve their own neuroses and peculiarities, let alone be capable of truly helping others with their lives – counseling can make matters worse. (The substitution of counseling or even psychotherapy for human warmth and contact was epitomized by a billboard I recently saw in a western state advertising the services of a local psychiatrist. It went something like: "No one cares? Well, I care!" Sure, but I couldn't help wondering how long that caring relationship would last if the client were to stop paying for the good doctor's time.)

Although I'm probably about average in my psychotherapeutic abilities, I just couldn't justify charging my private practice patients the going rate for the therapy that I was doling out. Sure, evidence-based treatment for, say, anxiety and depressive disorders can be quite effective when provided methodically and skilfully by a qualified clinician to a motivated patient.

And if a third-party payer, such as a workers' compensation board or automobile or health insurer, is footing the bill for treatment, it's justifiable and cost-effective. But charging someone $250 per 50-minute hour to listen to them, provide them with comfort, human companionship and semi-structured guidance and opinionated advice? I have my doubts.

Defensible in the case of a fully qualified psychologist or psychiatrist treating a serious disorder such as depression, trauma or anxiety, where the research has shown that evidence-based treatment such as cognitive behavioral therapy can be as effective as medication.

And defensible in the case of a truly exceptional therapist/human companion, with an intrinsic capacity for compassion and the ability to effectively communicate guiding wisdom. Not reasonable, in the case of most of the counselors and many of the psychiatrists and psychologists hanging out their shingles and handing out their sometimes-questionable prescriptive advice. I have certainly known a few so-called therapists from whom I would be highly reluctant to accept even free advice, and instead would encourage them to get themselves fixed before they try to fix others.

I'll conclude this line of discussion by noting that when it comes to the judicial and correctional world, it's been my experience that counseling or treatment for various types of offenders usually hasn't been particularly or at least universally productive, in large part because it's been based on the erroneous belief that if the offenders only could see the error of their ways they'd be motivated, and therefore able, to implement the required changes in their thinking and behavior.

Such beliefs certainly do not apply to many offenders. Nevertheless, when done appropriately, and given to those who are truly motivated for and capable of positive personal change, there are times when counseling and psycho-educational programs can be effective in improving the person and lowering the risk of recidivism.

Eventually, almost all inmates are released, and thus even from a self-serving perspective we should try to make them better (and certainly no worse) people before they are returned to our midst.

Chapter Five
Pupils, Priests, & Porn

Teacher's Pet

The evidence-based and relevant counseling discussed in the previous chapter was not available for Anita, a sex offender who I had the pleasure of meeting and assessing on behalf of the regional probation service. Had such counseling existed, it's likely that, being an articulate and well-educated teacher, at least in theory she might have been in a fairly good position to benefit from it.

That would assume, of course, that Anita saw herself as having any kind of difficulties in need of fixing and was motivated to address and hopefully remedy any identified causal problems – or what those of us in the business like to call "criminogenic (causing criminal) variables".

The trouble was that Anita, a high school teacher who had been convicted of sexual exploitation for having an intimate relationship with one of her teenaged male students, didn't see herself as having a problem. To her way of thinking, she'd been justified in having a sexual relationship with her student because he had flirted with her, she cared for him, and she was quite sure that he had feelings for her.

Disregard the major difference in age (she thirty, he around seventeen). Disregard the colossal violation of trust and ethics. Disregard the huge power imbalance and at least the potential for psychological/emotional coercion. And certainly, disregard any conflicts of interest: she wanted him and that was enough for Anita to justify and rationalize her sexual involvement with her student.

When I saw her for assessment Anita was polite but reserved. She informed me that in fact she had been pursued by her adolescent student-lover, who she said had expressed his attraction to her from the time of their first encounter in the grade eleven class she was teaching at the time. The age difference hadn't troubled her and probably had further attracted her to him, as suggested by the fact that by golly she'd already had sex with a teenaged friend of her victim.

This previous sexual encounter with a teenager was a huge red flag, providing a window into Anita's thinking, sexual interests and emotional maturity, and underscoring her willingness and capacity to sexually exploit a juvenile.

Anita was sufficiently intelligent and insightful to recognize that the loss of her teaching certification and her job had been technically justified, but at the same time she was sufficiently self-absorbed, immature, and narcissistic to believe that she shouldn't have been criminally charged. If the genders had been reversed, there would not have been too much support for the position that an adult male teacher who'd had a sexual relationship with one of his female adolescent students, and one of her teenaged friends before that, shouldn't have been charged because she'd flirted with him first.

The teacher-student relationship, like the doctor-patient one, is based upon a power/authority – as well as, in most teaching cases, a significant age – imbalance. As such, it's fitting to deal with any sexualized interaction within that dyad as promptly and efficiently as possible, to provide specific sanction and general deterrence and thereby lower the potential for similar future violations of trust and legality.

For these reasons, it was highly inappropriate as well as unethical and illegal for Anita to have had a sexualized relationship with one of her students. It represented a major exploitation of someone with whom she was in a position of trust and toward whom she had a duty of care. Some might argue that at seventeen the youth (who in most jurisdictions legally still would be considered a child) should have been able to enter into a consensual sexual relationship with Anita: she clearly believed that to have been the case.

Nonetheless, it's society's position that relationships such as the teacher-student, doctor-patient and clergy-parishioner ones are sacrosanct, and that those who violate the ethical boundaries and trust inherent in the dynamics of those associations should be sanctioned. Unfortunately, Anita remained unconvinced that she had behaved inappropriately, let alone illegally – which I suppose is not really surprising because her intransigence exemplified the kind of faulty thinking that had landed her in trouble in the first place.

And indeed, such violations keep on happening. It's almost become a routine occurrence for a teacher to be investigated and charged for having had a sexual relationship with a student. It's as if those teachers are overcome by their hormones and their desire for sexual and emotional gratification and are sufficiently egocentric to believe that they are different, that they will not get caught, and that the targeted youngster and his or her friends won't tell anyone about their illicit liaison.

I suspect that a combination of immaturity and a sense of entitlement and self-reference underlies many cases in which a teacher or someone in a similar position has satisfied their own needs by way of an inappropriate relationship. In addition, a small percentage of offending teachers will have a primary sexual interest in children or teenagers and will selectively target such youngsters: in those cases, the sexual interest may have been one of the reasons they were attracted to the teaching profession in the first place.

Although Anita's offense had dynamics that were different from those in many sex offenses, she was a sexual offender, and she was supervised as such. She received no sex offender-specific treatment, mainly because at the time such treatment simply did not exist for female sex offenders. Although the gender gap is narrower today than even a decade ago, the vast majority of sexual offenders are males.

It has been estimated that currently only about five percent of known sex offenders are female, and it's believed that the dynamics of female sex offending and the risk of re-offense may differ significantly from those of the male sex offender (sexual recidivism rates being lower for females than males, for example.)

With the expanded and changed roles of females in western societies, it's entirely possible that in the future there will be an increase in the relative numbers of female sex offenders. Anecdotal reports also suggest that a number of sexualized incidents perpetrated by females go unreported. Nonetheless, and despite the blurring of gender identities that has become fashionable during the past few years, I've been reliably informed that males and females differ from one another not only in terms of their socialization, and specifically their sexual socialization, but also in terms of their hormones and anatomies. For whatever reason – revolving around the fact that most guys are driven by having a great deal more testosterone than most girls, and that the phallus protrudes pendulously, acting as a perpetually perky and sometimes perplexing source of sexual stimulation, especially during adolescence and young adulthood – it's safe to say that males do focus upon sex quite a lot.

This sexual focus, and the associated psychological and biological imperative to satisfy sexual arousal, gets the guys into trouble much more frequently than it does the gals.

Despite what some may claim (some radical proponents going as far as to assert that any sexual interaction between males and females is exploitative and abusive of the female), in my experience sexual exploitation and coercion does not stem only or primarily from a gender-based power imbalance, a patriarchal sense of male entitlement, or purported toxic masculinity.

Although feelings of entitlement and coerciveness certainly do exist in some males (more so in some cultures than in others), intrinsic biological imperatives also are at play. There is of course considerable overlap between males and females, and libidinous similarities are likely to exceed the differences, but the human male sex drive does appear to differ qualitatively and quantitatively from that of the human female. Particularly during adolescence, the male libido can be all-consuming and overpowering.

But let's leave discussion of such tricky matters for another day, lest we stray too far into murky waters in which I will find myself being pilloried and drowned by angry social media mavens.

Suffice it to say that for whatever the reason – be it cultural, libidinal, or attitudinal – I've only seen about half a dozen female sex offenders for assessment, versus a thousand or so male sex offenders. One of those young females acknowledged having a pedophilic interest in prepubescent boys, that attraction also having become apparent when she was evaluated with an objective measure of sexual interest.

Another woman, in her mid-twenties, had offended against pre-pubescent males but claimed that her primary sexual attraction was to physically developed males, not pre-pubescent ones – as a testament to which she had a same-age common-law boyfriend at the time of her offense. In both cases, the women were of low intelligence and had come from difficult or unstable backgrounds. And as with their male counterparts, they showed a tendency to deny responsibility and to project blame onto others, including their prepubescent victims.

Pedophilia (defined as intense and recurrent sexual urges towards and fantasies about prepubescent children), as well as hebephilia (a strong, persistent sexual interest in early adolescents) and ephebophilia (sexual attraction to mid-to-late adolescents) certainly was a possibility in the above cases.

In the previously discussed situations, it's also likely that the ladies' immaturity and intellectual limitations played a causal role in their offending, making them more inclined to gravitate toward younger boys who they could exploit to satisfy their sexual needs and, being immature themselves, with whom they could relate.

Although both young women were found to be at elevated risk for future offending, neither of them received specialized counseling and instead were only carefully monitored. The availability of such specialized treatment resources for women may change in the future, depending upon whether there's a sizable increase in the number of identified female sex offenders – there has already been a rise in the number of programs available to women who have been convicted of physical assault and other offenses. Equality of opportunity and gender equity, I suppose.

An Unholy Father

Despite their notoriety and the attention paid to them and their carnal misdeeds by the media, I've only ever seen one Catholic priest sex offender in a professional capacity (my profession, not his). When I met with him, Father David was coming to the end of his probation term, having been monitored during the preceding three years. The supervising probation officer was interested in learning how the priest was doing, risk-wise, and if there was anything in particular about him that should be noted.

The most memorable thing about my encounter with this man of the cloth was that, despite having had the benefit of numerous chats with his probation officer – who happened to be a woman of the Catholic faith who had struggled with the inherent cognitive dissonance of it all – he remained querulous and decidedly recalcitrant in his attitude toward the justice system.

Indeed, with what in a less holy man might have been construed as a sneer, Father David defiantly and testily informed me that if he were to become aware that another priest was sexually abusing someone, he would certainly not report it to the authorities.

Although such a position was not at all unusual at the time (the late 1990s or shortly thereafter) and was reflected in the church's standard operating practice of closing ranks and transferring problematic priests rather than imposing any direct or explicit sanction on them, his stance epitomized the faithful father's feelings of entitlement and resistance. At heart, he believed himself to have been wronged and aggrieved.

Indeed, Father David conveyed a sense of self-righteousness and indignation that has lingered in the murkier corners of my mind. Perhaps understandably, he was quite vexed about the indignity of having been identified and punished as a sex offender. And despite his alleged dedication to the tenets of his religion and his ostensible commitment to the well-being of others, he communicated not only a whopping dose of defensiveness but also a stated willingness to protect other sexually offending priests (and thereby not protecting their victims) by not reporting their behavior.

I found this to be an interesting confession from him, and a failure of the justice system as well as the church to fix his faulty thinking. Judging by his attitude, I would also be inclined to bet that his risk was every bit as high at the end of his probation as it was at the beginning – perhaps even more so.

Although by then he was getting on a bit, and an aging body and diminishing sex drive – together with the knowledge that nowadays disclosure of abuse is much more likely than it was back in the good old days – are key factors that are likely to lower the risk of sexual re-offense.

Father David was a touch petulant, abrasive, and some might even say obnoxious regarding the fact that he'd been outed as a sex offender and now was being administered the further indignity of having to see a forensic psychologist. However, a majority of the sex offenders I've seen have not been so touchy (for some reason when referring to sex offenders, use of the words 'touchy' and 'prickly' doesn't seem quite right, but you get the idea); for the most part they've been able to at least pretend to be experiencing some pangs of contrition.

That said, it's not at all unusual for convicted sex offenders to continue to deny their guilt for some time after being convicted – sex offenders, like most people, tend to be a bit awkward when it comes to their sexuality, and often feel quite embarrassed about the nature of their offense.

Undeniably, as a society we are terribly conflicted about sex and what we want to do about it. At a time when nudity and sexuality in the media have never been more explicit and prevalent, and in an era in which we dress even young children in adult-style clothing, thanks to the feminization of western society (which has increased our emphasis on safety) and a number of well-publicized sexual and related offenses against children, we've become much more highly focused on the security of our children.

And as noted above, even though the teens of today are more jaded and mature and have been exposed to hardcore pornography and other explicit sexuality as never before, children usually are defined legally as being anyone under the age of eighteen. We have become extremely sensitized to the notion that adults sexually exploit children and that our children therefore must be protected – even as our children from a very early age have become desensitized to graphic sexuality.

Collectively, we revile sex offenders, particularly those who target children, and the term 'pedophile' has become synonymous with 'scum of the earth.' Such descriptors even extend to those whose only offense was the possession of child pornography (known in the policing and legal business as 'CP').

Now, before we launch into a discussion of a couple of CP cases, I must emphasize that there are some extremely dangerous people out there, and that some of those perilous people are sexually attracted to kids and have no qualms about doing some very, very nasty things to them. There are also some organizations or groups whose raison d'être is to access and market children for brutally exploitative purposes.

We're talking about kidnapping, forcing young children into sexual acts with adults and with each other (often for still and video recording and distribution), and sometimes even murder.

That's why organizations such as the National Center for Missing and Exploited Children exist. And why it's commonly believed that anyone who simply accesses and views CP is indirectly contributing to the victimization of kids.

And why the sometimes very challenging task and heavy responsibility of the forensic psychologist is to try to figure out which of the CP offenders have drifted into CP out of a quest for, for example, novelty and stimulation – and who aren't preferentially attracted to children (or who in any case would not be inclined to directly victimize a child) – and which of those offenders do potentially pose a direct threat to our children.

The Terrible Teens

The most extreme example of our severe societal reaction to any hint of the sexual exploitation of children, and what I believe to have been an example of puritanical zealotry on the part of law enforcement and the criminal prosecution department, was Tim.

Tim was a 16-year-old boy whose offense was that he'd received on his smartphone a photograph of one of his female peers, who just happened to have been (voluntarily) naked at the time the photo was taken. Tim's felonious mistake was that he had forwarded the image to some of his male friends. Boys, it has been said, will be boys.

Not only was Tim charged with the possession of CP – he was charged with the distribution of CP, which of course is even worse in terms of condemnation, shame, and sanction. Although with the help of his parents, who were able to foot the sizable legal and associated (ahem, psychological consultation and assessment) defense bills, Tim was able to avoid serious criminal consequences.

However, now he has a juvenile criminal conviction for an act that was undertaken without felonious or harmful intent – and quite frankly was something that many a young guy (and girl) has at least considered doing.

Sure, it was a thoughtless and crude thing to do, but to my mind it certainly didn't capture the spirit of the child pornography and child protection laws and should have been dealt with in an extrajudicial fashion – a stern warning from the school and/or law enforcement authorities would have sufficed as punishment and deterrence in Tim's case.

I've talked to and assessed a lot of men who've been convicted of CP offenses, and I've found few of them to have been pedophiles (which again is a primary and compelling interest in the immature child's body shape) or to have been at high risk for offending directly against a child.

Most of the guys I've seen who found themselves facing CP charges began by viewing mainstream forms of online pornography, usually featuring adult females; over time their quest for novelty and

86

stimulation inexorably led them toward more niche forms of pornography, culminating in hardcore CP.

Despite the increasingly sophisticated and pervasive monitoring of online activity by the police, the guys who get caught for possessing and/or distributing CP usually are the ones who shared inappropriate images with others, often through one of the readily available shareware programs. Particularly when one CP guy has been identified, and especially when he's been persuaded to cooperate, this can enable the law enforcement authorities to track the internet addresses of others who are accessing and sharing CP via the shareware application.

Given today's ability to download groups of files at extremely high speeds, it's not at all unusual for such guys to have accumulated many thousands of CP images on their computers. Not that long ago, I assessed a guy who had more than 15,000 CP images and over 1,000 CP videos, as well as over 300,000 child-related images, on his computer and storage devices: a relatively high number but by no means a record-setter (imagine being the unfortunate cop who was tasked with going through all of the offensive material, collating and describing it for the police report).

Sometimes the images can be relatively tame – girls and boys at the beach in their swimsuits or otherwise in various stages of undress, for example – but often the images are of an extreme nature: children posed nude and provocatively, and in the most horrendous cases being raped and otherwise subjected to heinous abuse.

Even the descriptions of these images in the police reports can be disturbing, and really make you wonder about the basic humanity of individuals who would treat vulnerable young beings in such a manner.

Sometimes, as in the case of the CP hoarding fellow referred to above, the guy hadn't even looked at most of the material he'd accessed and had simply batch downloaded the files. Although I've had men tell me, with apparent candor, that they really didn't like the more explicit and extreme imagery and had deleted it when they'd seen what it was all about, the fact that they were involved in the distribution of such images is considered to be (usually indirectly) abusive of the children in those pictures: it perpetuates the manufacturing of CP, and thus the exploitation and victimization of youngsters. At least, that is the stated rationale behind the laws which forbid the possession of such imagery.

Of all the guys I've tested for sexual interest after they'd been convicted of possessing and distributing CP, only a handful have tested positive for a pedophilic disorder: this finding generally was consistent with their backgrounds and with their contention that they'd accessed the CP primarily out of curiosity and a quest for something novel and titillating.

If the guy has no history of sexual offending and there are no other indicators of risky or antisocial behavior, the danger of him going on to commit a contact sexual offense against a child or an adult is likely to be in the low range.

For such reasons, an argument can be made that the simple possession (and sometimes distribution, if the fellow had not been actively and deliberately disseminating the material) of CP shouldn't be penalized as harshly as a sexual offense in which there is an identifiable victim. Certainly, from a diagnostic perspective the individual should not automatically be considered to be a pedophile.

However, given our current levels of enhanced vigilance and protectiveness regarding our children, our propensity to view anyone who has incurred any kind of sexual charge involving a child as a pedophile, and our present inclination to view masculinity and male sexual behavior as a whole in a somewhat dubious light, this distinction is a tricky one to argue, even within the confines of the ostensibly genteel gladiatorial courtroom arena.

Also, as we discussed earlier, there are some unbelievably bad and dangerous individuals and organizations in the world motivated to abduct and viciously exploit children, and often those entities are directly involved in the manufacture and distribution of CP.

It seems to me that some of these people derive perverse satisfaction not only from the sexual mistreatment of children but from obliterating the children's innocence.

So, to use a bad fishing metaphor, although we shouldn't treat the minnows in the same way that we treat the sharks, and we need to figure out which is which, we also need to ensure that the sharks aren't getting fat with the help of the minnows. Take away the market and you take away the marketer. The problem is that, thanks in large part to the internet, the market still seems to be growing.

Like the cases referred to above, Sol was the kind of guy who was unlikely to pose a direct threat to anyone, adult or child. Nevertheless, because he'd collected, viewed, and shared CP, he'd generally be considered to be someone who had indirectly victimized children and therefore deserved punishment.

I saw Sol a few years ago, during a period when there'd been a considerable increase in the societal, and therefore law enforcement, interest in tracking and seizing anyone who had accessed CP. As mentioned, typically but not always the guys who got caught were those who had been both downloading and uploading CP.

Most of the time, such distribution was made possible via the so-called dark web, together with use of one of the peer-to-peer (P2P) file sharing software programs which enable an interested party to access and download files, and by default permit others to view and download the files present on their computers.

Pursuing and identifying the end-user CP seekers, although by no means a law enforcement slam-dunk, and often requiring a hefty investment of police resources, has become easier as technology has evolved; and judging by some of the characters I've met, sometimes has been a bit like catching mentally slow fish in a barrel, using a large net backed up by a shotgun.

And many fellows have been netted by such trolling methods, dragged to the surface, identified, and churned through the naming and shaming mulcher. In some cases, they'd quickly progressed to being suspended or fired from their jobs, if their work brought them into contact with children or others who could be at risk for victimization (and the definition of such risk can be quite variable and expansive), or simply because they'd been caught and charged with a sexually related offense.

Sol was a lonely and sad man who had been caught by local law enforcement in just such a manner. He was in his late fifties, and as a semi-skilled manual laborer whose job did not bring him into contact with children or anyone else who might be vulnerable, he was still working full-time. However, he spent most of his days and nights in complete isolation: during the week he worked pretty much alone and went straight home; on weekends he stayed home and on Mondays he went back to work.

Sol had little or no meaningful social interaction. Although he had enjoyed several consensual sexual relationships when he was in his late teens and twenties, for many years he'd had no intimate associations whatsoever. A long time ago he had been married for a while, and even had a couple of kids to show for it, but for well over a decade he'd had no contact with either his ex-wife or his children.

As a child, Sol had witnessed domestic violence, with both mom and dad periodically assaulting each another. Also, on three occasions and by three different guys, he had been sexually molested. Otherwise, his background had been normal prior to his adjudication on charges related to the possession and distribution of child pornography.

Well, not entirely normal. There was also the small matter of his previous compulsion to expose himself: this earlier habit had resulted in him being convicted of indecent exposure when he was in his early twenties, which had contributed to the demise of his marriage.

From a psychodynamic perspective, Sol's negative experiences as a child may have generated a variety of psychological conflicts, including his inability to skillfully handle and express his emotions. Most of the 'indecent actors' (as the exhibitionists tend to be called in legal lexicon) who I've met have had some sort of pivotal experience during their formative years that launched their exposing careers, and Sol was no exception.

Although he still had no idea why he'd previously felt compelled to encourage females to look at his genitals, it was clear that the sexual stimulation associated with such exposure had become rewarding in its own right, and that the habit had proven to be extremely difficult for him to suppress – even at the cost of his marriage.

Frankly, I doubt that he ever did fully control his urge to exhibit himself. It seems, however, that over the years – as Sol had aged and his sex drive had aged with him – he'd felt less and less of a need to expose his privates and more and more of a need to retreat into private pornography perusal and self-pleasuring. As he put it when talking to me, with the internet there was simply no need for him to go anywhere, anymore.

No need to go anywhere that is, until he had received a call from the police, who had invited him to visit them for a wee chat. After which one thing had led to another, and Sol had ended up pleading guilty to charges related to the possession and distribution of CP. Although he hadn't actively been distributing the porn, the fact that it had been made available to others via the P2P software on his computer had rendered him technically and legally culpable for its distribution.

Being prone to depression, Sol became suicidal after he was charged, but never acted on his self-injurious impulses. But even though he wasn't actively suicidal when I met him, he was really down on himself, referring to himself as a pervert and appearing to genuinely want to improve himself and control the demons that had controlled him throughout most of his adult life.

During the clinical interview, Sol admitted that he found older pre-pubescent and adolescent females to be sexually attractive. He admitted to masturbating to images of girls, and although he denied being attracted to the younger kids, he conceded that he did find them sexually alluring but just didn't want to believe it.

Unlike many child porn guys, Sol hadn't simply sought out pornographic images of children in a quest for something new and forbidden and exciting, like the drug addict who requires increased amounts of a substance to get the same high (known technically as tolerance and habituation). He also revealed that similar to an addiction, he'd been downloading pornography for many years, and that his use of porn had become both compulsive and excessive.

In Sol's case it was apparent that he could specifically be sexually aroused by children – a fact which he realized may have been connected to his own childhood sexual abuse. For the assessing psychologist, such attraction raised the stakes when it came to figuring out whether – particularly given his prior history of exhibitionism – Sol was at significant risk for progressing to any sort of contact sexual offense.

Working in Sol's favor when it came to dangerousness was the fact that he found his attraction to kids to be personally repugnant, that he was at least intellectually aware that the children in the images were being exploited and harmed, and that despite the nature of his charges he really didn't want to do anything that might cause harm to a child.

On examination, Sol wasn't found to be suffering from any sort of major mental disorder. He was of average intelligence and okay on a cognitive level. Not surprisingly, he was quite a fragile fellow, prone to feelings of sadness, anxiety, self-doubt, and alienation from others.

There was also a degree of underlying anger and restlessness in Sol that had its roots in his adverse childhood experiences: his sexual abuse in particular seemed to have affected him quite a bit; the irony of course being that now he was charged with having indirectly promoted the sexual victimization of other children, by way of his prodigious use of child porn. (Incidentally, a disproportionate number of sex offenders have been sexually victimized as children, although such abuse is neither a necessary precursor nor an excuse for their victimization of others.)

As a component of my assessment, I ran the AASI computerized sexual interest test on Sol, and the results were entirely consistent with his own report. Objectively, he showed a significant degree of sexual interest not only in female adults and older female teens (both of which are biologically/psychologically normal areas of attraction for adult heterosexual males) but also in girls aged between six and thirteen.

Thankfully, the test results didn't suggest an interest in girls aged five and under. So, it turned out that Sol was sexually attracted to females from mid-childhood upwards.

Actuarial rating of Sol using the Static-99R put him in a risk category that was in the 'average' range. Statistically, that meant that over the next five years those in his risk range would have a sexual re-offense rate of around four percent. So, on average over the next five years about four out of one hundred male sexual offenders with a similar risk profile would recidivate sexually.

Most people think that most if not all sex offenders are at substantial risk for sexual recidivism. In reality, the probability of such re-offense – bearing in mind that we're only talking about the rates of known recidivism – is quite low, and even in the highest risk groups the re-offense rate seldom goes above fifty percent: high, to be sure, but not nearly as high as many people are inclined to believe, given the notoriety, fear, and loathing associated with sex offenders.

As such, Sol was not at especially high risk, and also working in his favor were his ability to recognize his shortcomings, his willingness to take responsibility for his actions, and his sincere desire to do better. He was already seeing a therapist and he was deriving some benefit from his involvement in counseling related to his offending and overall psychological functioning.

He'd also started to attend church services – such attendance being good for him, if only as a means of promoting appropriate social interaction. Of course, as in most similar cases, one of my recommendations was that Sol shouldn't tempt fate (or himself) by being alone with girls or teens, so there would be a need for him to exercise caution and good judgment in his interaction with the members of the congregation.

I didn't think that Sol needed to go to jail from a remedial or protective perspective, but the laws being what they are, and factoring in specific and general deterrence, he was guaranteed to receive some jail time.

As it turned out, Sol did receive a sentence that included a period of imprisonment, as well as a subsequent term of probation. The good thing was that he got to serve his sentence 'intermittently' on weekends, which meant that he was able to keep his job, pay his taxes, and try to move on with what remained of his life. Under the circumstances I think that the chances of Sol getting into further trouble are quite low.

Now, had Sol been twenty rather than pushing sixty, I might have thought otherwise; but at his age, and given what he'd been through in terms of legal fees, time in court, and weekend incarceration followed by community supervision – all superimposed on his personal feelings of repugnance regarding himself and his sexuality – his risk was relatively low. But never say never, especially when it comes to sexual offenders.

From a technical perspective Sol was a sexual offender not so much because of his CP possession and distribution offense, which is considered to be a lesser, adjunct form of sexual offense, but because of his previous conviction for indecent exposure. This prior offense was of course taken into consideration when calculating his risk level.

And indeed, the last I heard he was still at work and staying out of trouble. I hope not to hear about him again. I confess to having had a bit of a soft spot for old Sol: he was quite a forlorn and lonely character who, despite some underlying angst and anger, was not at all mean or nasty. But he was sufficiently troubled both behaviorally and psychologically to warrant monitoring as a sexual offender.

No discussion of libidinal loopiness would be complete without discussing Ralph, a gentleman who was reporting to the specialized (sex offender) probation office to which I was consulting once a week and in which I had previously seen Anita the teen teacher and Father David the pedophilic priest.

As someone who is an animal lover (platonic lover, I should add, given the nature of our previous discussion of Phil the Horseman), the details of Ralph's offense were simultaneously intriguing and appalling to me. I'll briefly outline Ralph's case to illustrate the fact that anything and everything can be sexually alluring to someone, somewhere, sometime.

Ralph's modus operandi, at least when it came to the behavior that resulted in him being put on probation, was to take a dog (a German Shepherd, no less) and dress it in women's underwear. Now, I know exactly what you're thinking: a French poodle looks so much better in lingerie than does a German Shepherd – a wee dab of perfume behind those pointy little poodle ears, and you're off to the dance.

However, it's a well-known fact that there's really no accounting for taste when it comes to canines and their undergarments, and besides, it's beneath us to judge others merely on the basis of their taste in dog's dainties. At any rate, without digressing too far into the mysterious realms of animal underclothing, Ralph had been convicted of animal cruelty.

Because not only had he dressed the dog – he'd also killed it, hung it up and, yes, copulated with it. Nasty. The sexual nature of the offense, and the very real concern that if Ralph was capable of doing it to a canine there was a good chance that he was capable of doing it to a human, explained why he was receiving specialized sex offender supervision.

Ralph's case was interesting because of the jaw-dropping and appallingly weird nature of his offending behavior. There's a reason the term bestiality can mean either sexual intercourse between man and animal or particularly cruel or depraved behavior. But one of the reasons I raise it here was the reaction of the female probation officer who had been tasked with supervising and trying to be civil with Ralph.

The officer in question could manage the dynamics of the offense without too much difficulty – after a while even cases involving dead raped dogs in female undergarments, while admittedly reading a bit high on the strange spectrometer, become routine, and after all it was in her job description, and she'd volunteered for the position. The thing was, the probation officer was as a pooch owner and (platonic) lover herself, and as such she found herself to be in a bit of a predicament.

The officer was perfectly capable of setting aside her personal feelings about Ralph and his perverse pooch predilections and providing him with appropriate monitoring and supervision service. But every time that Ralph visited her office, the officer felt obliged to ensure that she took the framed photograph of her own darling doggie (a wee white terrier who went by the name of Georgina, as I recall) that took center stage on her bookshelf and turn it around so that it faced the wall.

Her concern being that Ralph would fixate on her pooch's portrait and lust after little Georgina. Stranger things have happened, and heaven only knows where that could have led. So, just as a mother bear defends her cubs against danger, so did the probation officer do her bit to protect gorgeous Georgina against Ralph's leering and lascivious longings.

Not a consideration for most mothers but then Georgina's mom wasn't your average mater and Ralph wasn't your average masturbator.

So, Ralph was kept on a tight leash, as it were, and he managed to make it through his probation term without any major difficulties. He never did get a chance to lust or go after Georgina, and her mother (who for some reason took early retirement from probation services) slept a little better at nights.

As far as I know and hope, Ralph has not re-offended – although just because I've heard nothing of him since that time doesn't mean that he hasn't destroyed other animals or humans along the way. Ralph had an unusual and disturbing fetish which mixed elements of zoophilia (an erotic interest in animals), with bestiality, sadism and necrophilia. A kinky sexual interest is perfectly okay if it doesn't cause harm to another person or animal. In Ralph's case, however, he'd crossed the line and had killed another sentient being in order to satisfy (temporarily – the lust always re-emerges) his extremely selfish and destructive desires.

We can clinically hypothesize that Ralph had acquired his sexual affinity for dogs at some point during childhood, likely because of some early sensitizing experience. But that doesn't alter the fact that he'd cruelly harmed an animal which presumably had been someone's pet and companion, for no reason other than to selfishly satisfy his sexual desires.

Something for us to ponder, the next time we see a "Dog Missing" poster. At least coyotes and cougars usually eat what they kill. Humans have that unique capacity to derive pleasure or perverse satisfaction from sexualized and other forms of cruelty. We the people can channel both the highest and the lowest of impulses, soaring to the heights of spirituality and creativity as well as to the depths of darkness and depravity.

Chapter Six
Murders Most Monstrous & Mundane

Broadly speaking, the many murderers I have met have fallen into three categories: those who killed by accident and/or while emotionally overwrought; those who killed out of expedience and/or practicality; and those who killed for pleasure and/or lust. Of course, there's a degree of overlap and blending between these types, as in the case of the lust-crazed and emotionally overwrought individual who murders his victim during a sexual attack to prevent later identification.

There is also the individual who kills while delusional – an example of this being provided below. But, in my experience with killers, these three classifications tend to represent the main murderous motivators. The following are accounts of just a few of the more memorable killers I've encountered.

Life Was a Gas

I assessed Patrick at the request of the parole board. Patrick fell into the category of the accidental type of killer, albeit with a dash or two of the expediency. Moreover, Patrick's killing of another young guy wasn't entirely accidental or incidental, given that he'd aimed his car at the victim while attempting to flee the gas station at which he'd just stolen $10 of gasoline. For some, life (other people's that is) holds little value.

The very unfortunate young fellow who got run over by Patrick – and subsequently dragged for a few miles, thereby ensuring that he was killed quite nastily and his body rolled into a gory ball – was the service station attendant who'd boldly and likely impulsively put himself in harm's way in front of Patrick's vehicle, in an attempt to prevent his departure.

The file on this case, which I reviewed prior to meeting with Patrick, was memorable to me because it contained a detailed description of the crime scene and a medical account of what had remained of the victim's body following its involuntary final journey beneath Patrick's car. Not something that the involved police, paramedics, or coroner will be likely to forget, I'll wager.

Patrick's actions were both callous and capricious – and even making allowance for the possibility of contributing elements such as panic, substance use, and psychological denial of what was happening at the time, the fact that he'd driven as far as he had with the victim's body beneath his car says something about his character and his relative capacity for compassion and cruelty.

Patrick hadn't set out to kill anyone that night, and in some respects the offense of manslaughter to which he pled guilty (after initially being charged with second-degree murder), was the result of a semi-spontaneous, partly accidental event. Still, he'd driven right at the attendant, and he'd done so while committing another crime. Also, he'd continued to drive long after he'd struck the attendant and had taken him along for the ride.

Heaven (or perhaps hell) only knows what was going through Patrick's mind as he motored along, with the occasional thump and a mushy feeling to the steering serving as periodic reminders of the dying and disintegrating human being gumming up his chassis. I suspect that the only reason that he did finally stop his vehicle was because elements of the victim's body had become wrapped around the car's axles and wheels, literally preventing him from proceeding.

It may therefore come as no surprise that when I finally got to meet Patrick – he'd previously failed to show for our first appointment, owing to his reluctance to arise from his bed for our 9 am appointment – he came across as a pretty cold and grumpy guy. Were I not attempting to be a consummate professional and were this not a book for readers of all sensitivities, I might even have been tempted to describe him as an inter-buttock orifice.

By the time I saw him, Patrick had spent several years in prison and had taken a variety of rehabilitative programs. Although there was no evidence of a mental disorder in Patrick, I rated him as being moderately high on old the psychopathy checklist. He certainly didn't seem to have internalized much, if anything, from the programs he'd taken in terms of insight, prosocial thinking, or even self-serving fake charm. In my estimation he had a good potential to continue his interrupted criminal career when he was released from jail, and to continue to selfishly exploit others for his own gain.

It was entirely up to the parole board as to whether he warranted early release, but I couldn't help thinking that, given the same circumstances, Patrick remained quite capable of behaving exactly as he'd done when he'd driven over and dragged the gas station attendant to his death. I hoped that increased maturity and experience would help to him to avoid trouble over the longer term, but he showed neither enhanced maturity nor remorse, and I doubted it.

A couple of years after my meeting with Patrick, and inconsistent with my recommendations to the board, he did manage to get himself released on parole. (I can only give my opinion, and I learned long ago to try not to let my ego get too involved when the decision-makers fail to heed my recommendations.) Reverting quickly to type, he proceeded to violate his parole conditions on several occasions, and consequently spent a few brief stints back in the pokey.

About five years after that he stole a car, and again found himself in the slammer for a bit, followed by a period of probation. Three years later, while still a young man, he was dead. The cause of his death remains unknown to me, but if I were to speculate, I'd say that he overdosed, experienced some sort of accident such as a car crash, or was murdered. A very tragic tale for all concerned, including the ill-fated Patrick, who on some level may have been profoundly affected by his killing of someone, particularly in such a manner. But an especially sad story for the gas station attendant whose life was painfully truncated, and for those who knew and loved him.

The End of the Affair

Further along the spectrum of killers and an example of the emotionally overwrought murderer, was Ivan, the guy I mentioned earlier who blasted away the lives of his wife and children with a shotgun. A similar type of killer was Ron, a guy in his early twenties who I met while he was in a pretrial center awaiting trial, albeit on a slightly smaller scale. Ron's conflict resolution skills also needed a bit of work, because he'd repeatedly stabbed, and thereby murdered, his former common-law girlfriend.

Some time before their final and fatal encounter, Ron and his erstwhile ex had experienced relationship difficulties, and she'd left him. Ron had not taken his beloved's departure at all well, and in what was very likely to have been an emotionally distraught state in which pique, panic, despondency and jealousy had figured prominently, he'd taken it upon himself to ensure that his erstwhile lady would have eyes for no one else.

As they say: act in haste, repent at leisure. And now Ron had all the time in the world with which to reflect upon his actions. Which is certainly more than could be said for his victim.

Ron had not had any previous contact with the criminal justice system and despite his recently demonstrated ability to wield a mean knife, he certainly wasn't a tough guy. Understandably enough, given the emotional maelstrom of the preceding few days and his sudden confinement to jail, he wasn't at the peak of happiness and mental stability when he entered the pretrial facility.

Primarily for his own protection, but also for the security of others (murderers or alleged murderers by definition being a bit unpredictable and violent) he was placed in the center's segregation unit, where he was on a restricted, small range in which inmates were confined to their relatively minuscule, metallic cells for most of the day and night.

Picture if you will a fairly slender (there's a reason why they call a knife *The Great Equalizer*, enabling as it does the little person to readily dispatch the big person), young and fragile fellow who'd recently killed his former girlfriend, who was in a state of shock and extreme desperation, and who had never before even visited a prison, let alone been locked up in one.

Confine that fellow to a small cell made entirely of reinforced steel, in which his contact with others was severely restricted (allowed out briefly to shower, with his interpersonal contact limited to a few words with the segregation unit guards) and you have a perfect recipe for rapid psychological deterioration – or what is referred to in the shrink industry as decompensation.

During his stay at the center Ron also was seen occasionally and fleetingly by the chaplain, the physician and one of the nurses on his or her rounds. But mostly he was left all alone with his thoughts, memories, and emotions. For most of us, especially those with normal sensibilities, a hellish scenario.

In an effort to mitigate his decompensation, and as a means of providing Ron with a measure of support and simple human (or as

Mrs. Manson has been known to say, somewhat simian) companionship, on several occasions I wielded my authority as the consulting psychologist at the pretrial center in order to have Ron escorted from his segregation cell to my office.

Despite this, before long he began to show signs of bats buzzing in his belfry, with low-grade auditory hallucinations (a voice speaking to or about him) and other indications of psychological slippage. This swift deterioration ensued from a marginally resilient individual being isolated during a period of extraordinarily high-stress immediately following a life-changing (and life-ending) event.

Now, although some may argue that Ron deserved what he was getting, we have to remember that technically Ron was innocent while he was awaiting the trial that would prove him guilty, and that in any case the judicial system requires defendants to be able to understand the court process and to be sufficiently *compos mentis* to instruct their legal counsel.

With a defendant who is descending into psychosis – unable to reliably distinguish so-called objective reality from the hallucinations and delusions of his mind – the possibility of him being declared "not criminally responsible" due to a mental disorder began to rear its head. Therefore, for both humanitarian as well as practical and legal reasons, it was important to keep Ron in as good mental shape as possible, given the circumstances.

I won't provide a complete account of Ron's tale here, other than to note that with the judicious use of medication and psychological intervention, Ron was stabilized and eventually able to traverse the trial process. He pled guilty to second-degree murder and had justice meted out to him in the form of a life sentence. The point of this account being to illustrate that Ron had been an unremarkable, friendly and seemingly gentle kind of guy until he was momentarily overwhelmed by his negative emotions. Then he translated those emotions into homicidal action. Such action resulted in the brutal and bloody termination of the life of someone for whom he'd previously cared and to whom at some point in their relationship he'd undoubtedly pledged his undying love.

Why is it that one emotion can generate its completely opposite emotion, even briefly? Love-hate. Like-dislike. Adoration-condemnation. Happiness-sadness. Hope-despair. Thumb up-thumb down. And so it goes, on and on – the emotional rollercoaster in our everyday waking and sleeping minds.

As with Ivan the Shotgun Man at the old prison, the clinical staff at the pretrial center did its very best to ensure that Ron didn't deteriorate significantly while he was being held for trial, and tried to ensure that his incarceration, together with the knowledge of the horrific deed he'd enacted, didn't drive him crazy.

Ivan and Ron were cases of the emotionally overwhelmed kind of killer, exemplifying the person who hadn't planned (or at least planned for very long) to commit murder, and had done so while in the thrall of the surging destructive emotions of anger, jealousy, fear, and sadness.

As those of us who have experienced momentary anger or its big brother rage know, once the emotion goes away, we can be left scratching our heads as to why we'd felt, acted and reacted as we had in the heated passion of the moment. Ivan and Ron had the rest of their lives to scratch their heads and contemplate what they had done and why they'd done it, while held captive by their all-consuming negative emotions.

Not a fate to be envied.

I never heard what became of Ron after he left the pretrial center. Although at some point, many years down the line, he would probably have become a reasonable candidate for some type of early release, by then his personality type would have guaranteed that he would have been thoroughly institutionalized and quite incapable of functioning adequately outside the highly structured prison milieu in which he'd always been told what to do.

Also, the knowledge of what he'd done to earn his incarceration would have remained with him for the rest of his days, undoubtedly burdening his spirit and weighing him down.

Barring, or even with, a wholesale spiritual conversion like the one Ivan had experienced when he'd found the Lord, such knowledge would have eaten away at Ron's psyche. If in fact he did return to the community, he would either have had to pour himself into some sort of cause, such as working with the needy and homeless.

Or, far more likely, he would have become a member of the marginalized. My bet is that if Ron ever were to have been let out of the regimented prison milieu and left to fend for himself, he would have struggled, stumbled, and fallen – turning to substances to help him to cope and to temporarily escape his mind.

For Ron, an opiate such as heroin or fentanyl would have done the job nicely. At major risk for addiction, homelessness, deterioration and early death, Ron served as another tragic example of how our momentary passions can irreparably alter the course of our lives – and abruptly end the lives of others.

The Lonely Leader of the Pack

Lorenzo also was an involuntary guest at the pretrial detention center at which I'd met Ron. Like Ron, Lorenzo was living the dream in the center's segregation unit. Unlike Ron, Lorenzo's placement in "seg" was for specific administrative reasons – namely, that he was the high-profile leader of a notorious criminal gang, and the pretrial brass didn't want him cavorting with other gang members. Or getting into a contretemps with rival gang members. Or otherwise fomenting unrest in the perpetually percolating inmate population.

Gazing back fondly as one does through the mellowing mists of bygone days, Lorenzo seemed like a decent enough, in some ways quite likable, guy who – I'm sure he thought through no fault of his own – just happened to have been charged with first degree murder after the sudden and premature death of a rival gangster.

Perhaps not surprisingly, at other times he'd also been charged with various other offenses, including attempted murder, assault, kidnapping, money laundering, and obstruction of justice. Indeed, Lorenzo and his lusty but loutish gang of loafers had been implicated in a diverse mix of assaultive and homicidal activity, as well as an assortment of other acts of lucrative criminality, such as higher-level drug trafficking.

I recall meeting with Lorenzo upon several occasions. He was a good chatter, and although I wouldn't say that we became best buds forever, we did have some decent discussions.

For a guy who was at the top of his game and gang, Lorenzo really didn't quite seem to fit the stereotype. For one thing, he was relatively young – still in his early thirties. He was of medium-large height and build, and although certainly not weedy, not a particularly huge, whacker type. He was clean-cut and wouldn't have looked out of place in a college classroom or local gym.

Immediately sensing my alpha manly and predatory advantage over him (we are allowed to dream), I was nevertheless all diplomat and discreet peacemaker with this homicidal gang leader.

Yes, it's true that, judging by his reputation and leadership role, Lorenzo was capable of exerting a macho commanding presence and being completely ruthless in the violence that he was reputed to have meted out. But I was a forensic psychologist. And I was packing a large pen.

In a documentary film that was subsequently made about Lorenzo, it was revealed that he was quite an outspoken gangster who, to put it mildly, was inclined to blatantly disregard societal rules and authority in all its forms. He was said to have been a bright kid and to have done well in school, but to have engaged in extracurricular activities such as seriously assaulting the vice-principal of his high school. Not surprisingly, at some juncture he had been diagnosed with an antisocial personality disorder.

Now he was the leader of a renowned criminal gang and had demonstrated a capacity to callously dispose of those who crossed him – for example by using a broken beer bottle on a couple of guys, and similarly assaulting and allegedly killing others. For all of that, the thing that stood out in my mind about Lorenzo, and the reason I bring him up here, is that for a mean and tough guy, he showed to me one whopping Achilles heel.

Lorenzo revealed his heel by whining and begging me on a couple of occasions to work my psychological magic to get him transferred out of the segregation unit. Now, although some may say that such pleading might have been manipulative (which is true), my assessment then, as it is now, is that in his case it was not: Lorenzo truly found being alone in his cell, devoid of human contact and distraction, to be intolerable.

Although capable of many things, Lorenzo was unable to be at ease all by himself, with only his own thoughts and feelings and the stillness and sameness of his cell to keep him company. Boring, yes, but also very frightening for him. If you recall the Coronavirus pandemic of 2020, think of life in seg as being a Covid lockdown on steroids.

Unfortunately for Lorenzo, as I mentioned he was in the segregation unit for security reasons. As such any recommendation that I might have made to the effect that when you got to know him Lorenzo was a sweet guy who deserved to be moved out of segregation, would have held little sway with the center's leadership. Also, as much as I might have liked Lorenzo (or at least not actively disliked him), even then I believed that it wouldn't have hurt him to learn something about consequences, as well as about himself, by having some time by himself.

Despite his distress at being deprived of social contact, I didn't consider his experience in seg to be likely to impinge significantly on his mental health, and in fact believed that eventually the experience could be beneficial for him.

Although longer periods of isolation now are often considered to be inhumane and therefore to be eschewed, and in a few regions even short periods of administrative segregation are discouraged if not explicitly prohibited, I believe that, like 'time out' for a child, brief periods of segregation can be both necessary and useful if deployed judiciously.

But segregation must be assigned humanely and carefully, and regular checks on the inmate's psychological and physical health should be incorporated into the segregation process.

As an aside, in some of the 'super max' prisons throughout the United States, inmates may be confined to their cells for 23 hours a day and have minimal interaction with anyone. One former resident of such an institution described the experience as being in a "special hell", in large part due to the sensory deprivation that's experienced by the isolated inmate. And it's no secret that, as in the case of Lorenzo, certain types of personalities have a lot more difficulty with such seclusion than do others.

Why can such isolation be so painful? Well, as most of us realized or rediscovered during the 2020 pandemic, humans are social creatures, and even the loner ("alone but never lonely, I'm perfectly happy sitting over here all by myself with my peanut butter sandwich") usually needs some kind of social interaction, even if it's only with his or her cat.

We simply do not do as well, and sometimes do very unwell, when deprived of social contact: we tend to become sick more easily and to die earlier when stripped of social interaction and support.

As I mentioned, this need for human connection is stronger in some people than in others, and in some of us the need is downright critical: these are the people who require a great deal of social communication to distract their minds, to fill the void, and to ensure that they aren't left all alone with just their thoughts and feelings to keep them company. For a majority of us, our daily lives are filled with all sorts of disruptions to 'just being' – by mixing and mingling with other people, by immersing ourselves in work, watching a movie, and by gazing interminably at our social proxies our busy-box smartphones. Keeping our minds busy and thereby staving off the existential loneliness, despondency and anxiety that can creep into our psyches when they aren't kept occupied and distracted.

Our minds can roam all over the place, but seldom are they at home by themselves. When our brains aren't playing away and being maintained in a dedicated state of preoccupation, the thoughts and feelings that we typically keep tamped down are free to bubble merrily to the surface. So, thoughts that revolve around issues such as failure, frustration, loss, loneliness, aging, and the death of ourselves and our loved ones can roam freely through our brains, generating sometimes overwhelming emotions of anxiety and sadness.

Fear is a big one for many of us, with most of us devoting a lot of our time and energy to consciously or unconsciously suppressing our worries and their cousin free-floating anxiety – often by pursuing diversionary strategies such as keeping ourselves busy and socializing. In some of us, alcohol and other substances serve a similar purpose. Cheers!

There's a good reason why some spiritual techniques revolve around meditation, solitary retreats and segregation from other people: the theory being that it's only by engaging in such isolation that we can identify the true nature of our minds and figure out who we really are and what it's all about.

The idea being that when our minds are filled with all kinds of thoughts, we're unable to focus and realize our true natures and the true reality of our world. For example, for many centuries adherents to some spiritual paths have partaken of dark retreats in which the individual, usually alone, remains in a secluded cave, room, or similar area in which all light has been excluded.

And I do mean all light. Pitch black. Complete darkness. The intention being that alongside such sensory deprivation can come insight (insight meaning seeing within rather than without – although sometimes in a dark retreat the retreatant also will see patterns or lights or shapes that seem to be 'outside' of what we assume to be ourselves) and other experiences that can promote spiritual growth.

Try it – you might like it! Then again, you might not: In addition to being all alone in such retreats, our fear of the dark is an inherent emotion, and absolute blackness, like absolute aloneness, can be absolutely unnerving for some of us.

So, such solitary pastimes certainly are not for everyone, and certainly not without preparation. And even people who've tried to meditate in broad daylight often will tell you that the first thing that they notice is how they can't stop thinking, and of how their thoughts really seem to pick up speed and become more intense, intrusive, and demanding of attention when they begin to meditate. It isn't that their thoughts are increasing, it's simply that they're becoming more attuned to them and aware of their insidious presence.

All of which is to say that being alone with our thoughts and fears can be a very daunting and even terrifying experience, especially for those of us whose personalities thrive on social interaction to keep our psychological ships on an even keel. I expect that this is particularly true for extraverted or gregarious individuals who like to talk and be talked to a lot.

Even seemingly high-achieving, strong, and resilient souls can grow faint of heart and falter when forced to stop what they are doing and just sit and quietly be alone with themselves. Without their smart phones.

Anyway, Lorenzo impressed me as just that kind of guy: a superficially strong character who could function well in social circles, was physically aggressive and capable, and felt at ease schmoozing with and dominating others.

He'd been quite successful in his workaday world, and the gang that he led was notorious and successful when it came to the territory it commanded and the illicit activities that were its bread and butter. But clearly, Lorenzo also was a fellow who needed to keep his mind full of this and that, and who didn't do at all well when cut-off from social distractions and other forms of diversion.

For him, being alone was a truly frightening experience – one of the few things that he really did fear.

Despite this fear, it was vital for Lorenzo's occupational success, and indeed his very survival, that he maintain his 'tough guy' persona. It was only in the privacy of my office at the pretrial center that he felt able to plead for his desegregation.

Prison is a special place when it comes to showing any form of vulnerability: Cry on the range in a male jail, and you're going to find yourself in a world of hurt. Many was the guy who shed tears in my office but who made very sure that the tears were all gone, and the eyes were neither puffy nor red, prior to swaggering back to be with the other inmates.

This was especially true for someone like Lorenzo, for whom showing any weakness – and particularly the panty-waist vulnerability of crying – would have been a career- and potentially life-ending mistake.

But not long after Lorenzo's pleas were pled and his tears were shed, he managed to get himself released from segregation. Indeed, he was granted bail and he left pretrial detention altogether.

Before you could say "slick lawyering" he was back on the street, commanding his troops and reaping the rewards, prestige, young women (just as there's a certain kind of guy who is attracted to gang membership, so there's a certain kind of gal who is attracted to a gang member) and other benefits of criminal gang membership.

Happy days were here again.

At least for a while.

I recall a particular scene from the hit television series *The Sopranos*, in which Carmela Soprano tells her husband Tony that "everything ends". Tony, American gangster boss extraordinaire but forever fifteen in emotional maturity years, had found this to be a novel and difficult concept to comprehend.

Being of a similar type to Tony, I expect that Lorenzo did too. But Carmela was right, for end it did. A year or so after our chats, Lorenzo was dancing his heart out at a nightclub in the wee hours of the morning, no doubt getting a buzz from the social contact and distraction for which he'd pleaded so earnestly in the pretrial center.

And then just like that, it all ended when someone came up behind him and gunned him down, catapulting him unceremoniously to that great nightclub in the sky. Or wherever.

Although Lorenzo died while surrounded by a whole lot of people, none of them proved willing or able to describe his killer. What's more, notwithstanding the crowd that encircled his dying body, he embarked upon his final journey from this life alone – as must we all, no matter how many people we're commanding and charming and no matter how many hands we're holding when we gasp our last ragged breath.

I hope that Lorenzo's passing was less painful for him than was the time he spent in the segregation unit. But somehow, I doubt it.

A Movie to Die For

I had the pleasure of meeting Wayne at a low-security camp that was situated on the outskirts of a forest, atop a small but very steep hill. (The road up the hill became quite treacherous in winter. I recall one fellow who worked there telling me how, one crisp and white winter's morning, the ice and snow on the unpaved and unplowed road had forced his car to a slick, sickening and wheel-spinning stop, whereupon his helpless vehicle had begun to inexorably slide, brakes locked, down toward the edge of the precipitous drop-off, stopping mere feet from what most certainly would have been a fatal fall.) Wayne had started his eight-year sentence several years earlier. Due to his age at the time, he had served his first few months in a youth prison – a haven which Wayne aptly described to me as "a breeding ground for criminals". When he came of age, he was transferred to a maximum-security adult prison, from which he'd gradually worked his way down ("cascaded" in correctional jargon) from max to min.

Doing good time, living the dream, and protected by his gang connections, Wayne was still in his twenties when we met. Indeed, Wayne had gotten a jumpstart on his career by committing his serious offense and beginning to serve big time when he was only eighteen. And what wickedness had Wayne wrought?

Well, Wayne had walked into a darkened movie theatre and had shot another teenager in the forehead. And although Wayne had left the theatre much more expeditiously (via a rear exit) than he'd entered it, he was identified by several witnesses (it was, after all, a theatre full of people whose eyes had adjusted to the dark), and he was quickly apprehended.

Now, the good and the bad news, depending on your perspective, was that Wayne had used a .38 caliber handgun to shoot the victim, who lo and behold was a member of a rival gang. The .38, being an under-powered and thus relatively pusillanimous caliber, had failed to extinguish its target's life.

The bad news was that although the target had survived, one of his eyeballs had not, and the excellent depth perception that he'd likely enjoyed prior to the shooting was gone once the bullet had breezed by his eyeball.

As an aside, at one point in my private practice I treated a fellow by the name of Rory, who had been shot in the face and had lived to tell the tale. I saw him on behalf of the regional worker's compensation board, to try to help him to resolve the trauma associated with the shooting and to adjust to and get on with his life as best as he was able.

Rory and I had something like six to eight sessions together, during which time I formed the opinion that he didn't appear to be suffering from PTSD (posttraumatic stress disorder), but definitely was angry about his disfigurement by the shooting, having had part of his lower face blown away.

Poor Rory had been providing door security at a nightclub at the time of the shooting, and he'd had some sort of negative interaction with a would-be patron. According to Rory, it isn't too difficult to jump the club line-up if you're willing to tip the guy at the door, but sometimes for whatever reason (such as the club being filled to capacity or the petitioning individual having a negative history at the club) someone can be categorically denied admission.

In Rory's case, the rejected patron had taken sufficient umbrage at having been excluded from the dancefloor that he'd stomped off to his car, pocketed his pistol, and assuaged his wounded ego by shooting Rory in the face. A bit hasty and some might say a slight overreaction, but there you are. At any rate, fortunately the assailant hadn't had particularly good trigger control and/or aim because his bullet had missed most of Rory's face, nevertheless succeeding in blowing off a big chunk of his jaw.

Frankly, I doubt that I was much help to Rory, who unfortunately now looked and sounded (his speech having been impaired by his reassembled but still misaligned jaw) dreadful and who understandably enough was quite exasperated and frustrated about what had been done to him.

What can you say to someone who has gone through such an ordeal, while still in his twenties, and who now had to live with its very noticeable consequences for the remainder of his days? I did my best with him, but Rory wasn't clinically depressed or specifically traumatized as such, and at the time there was little I could do beyond assessment, support, reframing, reassurance, and general attempts to get him re-established and moving forward with his life.

Rory was a feisty and resilient guy, and I suspect that eventually he did manage to get back on his feet. But of course, his life never would have been the same – as a testament to which, after he lost his good looks to the gunshot, he lost his live-in girlfriend, who left him.

And I expect that he lost all desire to resume nightclub security work.

But I digress. Because of Wayne's trigger control and sight alignment problems, the victim lost an eye rather than his life, and Wayne was convicted of attempted rather than first degree murder. Despite the blatantly homicidal and dangerous dynamics of his offense (discharging a firearm in a large, dark room full of people can be a wee bit risky to the public, even for those with good aim), Wayne was given a fairly light sentence.

Operating in his favor when it came to sentencing were Wayne's youthfulness and the fact that the victim also was a member of a criminal gang. In fact, Wayne's motivation for the offense had been that as a mere associate member of his gang, he had been 'earning his chops' – demonstrating his courage and fealty by taking a rival gangster out of circulation, in a public place no less.

Now, in the usual scheme of things being released from prison would be a good thing: even though you lose your three squares a day, the pluses tend to outweigh the minuses. We take our freedom for granted until we don't have it.

The trouble was that Wayne was not yet a citizen of this vast and free land of ours, and although he'd spent a majority of his life in this country, having come here with his parents as a young child, neither he nor his parents had bothered to take out citizenship papers for him. And now that he'd committed an indictable offense, he'd undeniably made himself eligible for deportation back to his country of origin – which in Wayne's case was a large Asian nation.

In fact, the immigration authorities already had been hovering around, initiating deportation proceedings and anxiously awaiting the opportunity to slap on the old manacles and provide him with a taxpayer-funded one-way plane ride back to the place from where he'd come.

Because there are various defenses in such cases (in this one, Wayne's age at the time of the index offense, his statistically low risk of recidivism, and his close ties with and support from his law-abiding family), as part of the immigration adjudication process a psychological assessment was requested.

That's where I came in. Fundamentally, these types of psych evaluations usually are focused on the amount of risk that the individual poses and related to that the chances of his or her future stability. Humanitarian factors, such as the effects on the offender's family and in particular children, often are a secondary but important consideration. In this case, although in his teens Wayne had flirted with delinquency by affiliating with a criminal gang, his index offense was his first.

Although Immigration assessments can quickly become routine, in my experience they're also about the closest that a forensic specialist can come to meeting 'normal' people in intact families – spouses and other family members, including children, whose lives would be directly affected by a deportation.

And Wayne's offense had some interesting aspects to it, given the nature of the actors involved and the dynamics of the behavior. I'd also imagine that it would have been quite stimulating from the bird's eye view of someone seated in the rows immediately adjacent to and behind the eyeball donor, who was munching merrily on his popcorn and mesmerized by the movie when he was treated to lead in the head.

Sadly (for those of us who thrive on the eccentric and the bizarre), from a forensic perspective Wayne proved to be a bit boring. Although apparently he'd mellowed somewhat during the time in which he'd been incarcerated, and now seemed to genuinely regret his homicidal behavior and its consequences, he reminded me of a slightly worn marine corps private: a loyal soldier whose primary qualifications for the job were his disinclination to spend a lot of time thinking about the ramifications of killing, his physical and psychological preparedness to complete the mission, and his deference to authority. Such qualities enabled him to do what he was told to do without asking questions.

Of course, Wayne's call to duty had not involved service to his country, but to his gang. There are a lot of differences but also a lot of similarities between military and gang service, at least when it came to foot soldiers like Wayne.

My evaluation of Wayne confirmed that he wasn't suffering from any kind of mental disorder. He had some antisocial aspects to his personality – he was after all a (supposedly former) gang member who'd attempted to commit a premeditated murder and as a result had spent several years in prison – but he didn't stand out as being someone who was especially ruthless, belligerent or unstable.

He wasn't into drugs or alcohol. He was of average intelligence. He came across as being capable of a degree of callousness, and his offense spoke of his capacity to behave in an uncaring fashion, but he wasn't particularly psychopathic: he didn't possess the immense egocentricity or the superficial charm and manipulativeness typically evinced by the dedicated psychopath. Nonetheless, he did strike me as a bit of a cool customer – which I suppose was one of the reasons he'd been assigned his murderous mission.

Wayne's greatest stability risk, based upon his demonstrated loyalty to a criminal cause and the perpetration of his offense, was that if ever he were to be released from custody, he could get into further difficulty by again becoming actively involved with his gang.

Although he was able to speak poignantly of his regrets regarding his immersion in the criminal/gang subculture and talk the talk about how he'd realized the error of his ways, I didn't really believe that he'd ever stopped having some level of involvement with his gang while he was doing time.

What's more, his status in the gang would have risen considerably precisely because of his offense and his demonstrated capacity to bite the bullet (although his victim came closer to physically doing so) by stoically embarking upon his sentence with nary a peep about his accomplices and other criminal associates (in part, no doubt because he knew very well what would happen to him if he were to 'rat them out'). I communicated these and other streams of consciousness in my report to the referring immigration lawyer.

The report was submitted, and I moved on, giving the matter no more thought. A few months later, not entirely to my surprise but always guaranteed to stimulate the adrenalin flow, I received a subpoena kindly demanding my presence to testify at Wayne's immigration hearing.

The immigration authorities weren't prepared to wait around until he was paroled and given an opportunity to disappear into the woodwork. They wanted him gone. I recall that during direct and cross-examination, much discussion and questioning revolved around the degree of Wayne's antisociality, whether he could be diagnosed as having an antisocial personality disorder, and whether his risk could be managed.

The immigration authorities were very keen to facilitate Wayne's return to his country of origin, and at the end of the day there wasn't a great deal that could be said to refute their assertions that he had relinquished the right to remain in this country.

He was therefore in the unenviable position of nearing the end of his custodial sentence with the knowledge that, barring some legal miracle, if he were to be released from prison, he would immediately be apprehended by immigration officers and further detained in anticipation of his removal from the country.

As such, Wayne was slated to join the ranks of the many people I've seen who had spent most or all of their lives in this great nation of ours, but whose criminal behavior had resulted in their deportation back to a country that they hadn't seen for a very long time, if ever, and with which they had little or no connection.

Not so bad, in comparative terms, for the guy I saw whose Hell's Angels affiliation, criminal associations, and various misdeeds resulted in him being returned to Italy. Not so good for other guys I saw whose criminality caused them to be sent back to places like Africa, Afghanistan, and Russia.

One of the hallmarks of many, but certainly not all, criminals is that they're not always particularly good at thinking through the consequences of their actions. It hadn't dawned on Wayne or the other criminals who got themselves deported that it would have been prudent for them to have gone to the trouble of acquiring their citizenship before embarking upon their criminal careers.

They never dreamed that they'd get caught, or at least that their immigration and residency status would become quite uncertain if they were to be apprehended. I'm sure that Wayne and his family would agree that the consequences of crime can be long lasting, for perpetrator as well as victim.

Our Eyes Met

Derek was a middle-aged, greying gentleman with whom I chatted upon several occasions while he was awaiting trial for first degree murder. Derek had no prior criminal record and he was something of an enigma. A hitherto ostensibly fine, upstanding citizen, one day he'd decided to take hold of a heavy implement and apply it vigorously and repeatedly to the head of one of his fellow citizens.

The result of this ostensibly headstrong (but as it turned out quite deliberate and planned) maneuver was that the recipient of Derek's skullduggery had received sufficient blunt head trauma to swiftly render him unconscious and then dead.

Although initially the motive for Derek's attack was unclear, because he and the dead dude hadn't known each other prior to the head-bashing event, it turned out that Derek had become peeved and aggrieved by the knowledge that the victim had been cavorting with a lady who had previously been the object of Derek's amorous desires.

The course of true love never did run smooth, and I guess that a man has to do what a man has to do.

In keeping with the fact that he had been charged with (and was later convicted of) murder, it can be reliably construed that Derek was a bit different from your average mild-mannered, middle-manager type. Yet he'd led quite an ordinary life prior to the murder and had attained a reasonable degree of success in terms of occupation, income and lifestyle.

That being the case, his presentation and charges implied that something had significantly changed in him. It was to say the least odd that Derek suddenly had decided that he didn't like the fact that his former lady friend had taken up with someone else and that therefore it would be a good idea for him to kill her new paramour.

Well, I suppose that thinking that he'd like to kill the new guy was one thing, but actually hatching a homicidal plan and carrying it to fruition is not in the mainstream middle class standard operating procedure manual. My clinical sixth sense hinted at the possibility that Derek was experiencing some sort of neurocognitive problem, likely because of injury or early-onset dementia. Derek was just strange enough to be mildly peculiar – and, as it turned out, murderous – but not odd enough to stand out in a crowd of bus riders.

And not unusual enough to seek exculpation on the grounds of insanity. In my estimation, Derek was, according to legal as well as clinical criteria, sane. But as technically sane as he may have been, there was an undercurrent of something different and chilling about him.

We've already talked about how there are all kinds of tests, scales, and clinical checklists with which to identify mental disorders and other variables of interest. But I've also relied heavily on my sixth sense when conducting assessments: although objectivity and science are great, at the end of the day we're humans interacting with other humans, and we all have an intrinsic ability to develop a gut feeling for the people we meet.

Although I've prudently resisted any urge to employ a crystal ball, tea leaves or entrails during my evaluations, it's been my experience that, despite its having fallen out of favor (in no small part because it can be difficult to defend a "hunch" as being anywhere near "evidence based" when testifying in court) clinical intuition is likely to be a good, albeit highly subjective, barometer for "what is going on with this person?" Functioning on a semi-conscious or subconscious level, this sixth sense may be conceptualized as an amalgamation of the innate, the learned, and the sometimes forgotten (from everyday working memory) bits and pieces, operating in holistic, ineffable and in our fact-based world mysterious ways.

You don't need to be a professional psychologist to have encountered this phenomenon: most of us have had the experience of feeling uneasy about a certain type of person, or conversely of experiencing an attraction to someone without knowing why.

On some level that individual is likely to remind us of someone else we've met and with whom we've had either a positive or negative encounter. Or perhaps we have some sort of biological prejudice against beady, closely set eyes (there's a reason why adorable puppies and successful movie stars usually have big peepers).

Of course, when it comes to writing a formal forensic assessment report, part of the skill lies in being able to convey opinions in an objective and ostensibly evidence-based manner: just writing something along the lines of "my gut told me he was no good" or "never trust a guy with a really big, red nose" isn't a great way to enhance one's reputation or to generate repeat business. And in Derek's case, this medium-height, fiftyish and greying geezer (much older than the average inmate) was superficially pleasant enough but had a 'creep factor' to him that was a touch disturbing. I wouldn't have wanted to have unnecessarily annoyed or agitated him, or indeed to have unexpectedly encountered him in the woods.

Despite such vibes, during a number of my chats with Derek we discussed a variety of issues and got along quite well. Nevertheless, my primary focus and real reason for seeing him had been to monitor his psychological status while he was in the pretrial center and to ensure that he didn't deteriorate or otherwise get himself or others into any sort of difficulty: being who he was, having a capacity to run off at the mouth, and being naïve when it came to the prison system, peer problems were a distinct possibility.

Of course, it also was quite interesting to speak with someone who was alleged to have had cold-bloodedly bludgeoned someone to death, especially for such a trivial reason. Oddly enough, given his otherwise normal background and appearance, Derek reminded me of the time that I was left alone with a large iguana by the name of Sully.

Now, anyone who knows me knows that I'm a sucker for animals: cats, for example, intuitively can see the writing on my forehead which reads: "Pussy Cat Pushover". And Sully had, at least to my knowledge, never eaten a human or taken particularly large, juicy chunks of their oozing flesh into his capacious chops (well, I'm told that he did do so once, but undoubtedly for a good reason and with good motivation).

Moreover, at the time that I went solo with Sully, I'd already been alone with many a murderer and miscreant. But I must confess that as Sully gazed unblinkingly at me from the sofa on which he was lying (and which he filled), something large and very cold strolled across my grave. My sixth sense was sounding a siren in the limbic system (also known as the reptilian area) of my brain, warning me that those coldblooded eyes and the pointy teeth just beneath them were sizing me up as a tasty snack.

As it turned out, Sully didn't have the opportunity to take a nibble – and, to give him credit, his scaly bad looks and ferocious visage might have been worse than his bite. And unlike Sully, on an outer or superficial level Derek was placid and unthreatening. But my senses screamed that there was something disturbing and dangerously Sully-like about him.

Which is why the thing that remains vivid in my memory regarding Derek is something that never has happened before or since. It went like this: He said something or other to me, and I said something or other to him. There was an implicit challenge or disagreement in our discourse, and voila! we had our *ad hominem* moment.

Our eyes locked. And they locked. And they remained locked. And they locked some more. And they continued to stay locked. Although time distortion is not unusual in such situations, we must have stared at each other for well over a minute – which, if you've ever tried one of those silly human-relations group exercises in which you're paired off with another participant and instructed by the facilitator to lock eyes with that person – is a really, really, really long time.

As this was going on, a light glowed dimly somewhere in a higher part of my brain, feebly flashing the alarm that I was currently engaged in a primordially challenging, threatening, and dominance-testing duel with a guy who had been charged with a brutal murder.

My inner child's sixth sense was screaming "Danger, danger, look away from the eyes, look away from the eyes!" But I just couldn't help myself. For some reason, I was feeling annoyed at Derek, and I was determined to show him who was boss.

And the thing is – I won. He finally averted his gaze and by doing so implicitly acknowledged my domination. We both knew it. Silly and childish, I know. But extraordinarily satisfying. My machismo moment. I don't think that I would have tried it with, say, Lonesome Lorenzo or Ken the Screwdriver.

But on that day, with that particular murderer, I was top cat. The chances are good that I should have seen a psychologist about such over-compensatory, childish, and inappropriate behavior. But it did feel good and for some reason it has remained in my memory as a singular experience.

At any rate, Derek was duly convicted of murder and to the best of my knowledge, some twenty-plus years on, he continues to serve a life sentence as he sails serenely into his upper senior years. He'll be well into his seventies by now, and if my hunch about a brain injury or dementia was correct, it's entirely possible that he's become completely detached from our reality, has died, or both.

Still, Derek lives on in my mind as a testament to my, capacity for impetuousness, recklessness, and I must concede, stupidity. Sometimes I give my head a shake and wonder how I've made it this far. But then, like a good steak, life can be bland without a bit of spice and a glass or two of vino.

Bill the Bricklayer

Unlike Derek – who, although not exactly warm and fuzzy or even mildly cuddly, was something of a 'crime of passion' type of murderer – Bill primarily was a blend of the 'accidental' and the 'expedient' killer. I had the dubious pleasure and privilege of meeting Bill for a parole assessment, our encounter taking place at the minimum-security institution to which he had finagled his way, after he'd served many years in both maximum- and medium-security facilities.

Indeed, at the time of our encounter Bill was a resident of the correctional work camp, located many miles from civilization but with no bars, gates or perimeter fencing, at which I'd previously met with Wayne, of movie-shooting fame.

Bill had served over twenty years of a life sentence that had been imposed for his murder of a 3-year-old girl. Back in the day, he'd taken a brick and used it to repeatedly beat the little girl about the head, thereby ensuring that she didn't make it to her fourth birthday party.

Oh yes, and prior to (or – who really knows except for Bill – during or after) bludgeoning the young child to death, he had raped her. Still, as I got ready to see him, I was sure that Bill would have a rationale for his actions, and that he'd do his absolute best to communicate this explanation to me and to let me know just how sorry he was, and how he'd changed for the better.

Never one to disappoint, Bill's account of his offense was that he'd been heavily intoxicated at the time of the incident, and that somehow he'd encountered the girl (who he'd never met before) in the hallway of the apartment building in which she lived. Bill had then taken the child to a nearby location, where he had proceeded to rape her. According to Bill, he'd beaten the girl with a brick only because she'd started to cry, and he'd been afraid that the noise she was making would attract the attention of passersby.

An interesting justification, and undoubtedly one that he'd been using all along: when push comes to shove, better to claim that you'd drunkenly, impulsively and fearfully beaten-in a child's brains, rather than to say that you'd done so, oh, I don't know, so that she couldn't identify you or in the throes of sexual lust. Either way, the very tragic result was the same: a very raped and very dead little girl.

In short, Bill acknowledged having deliberately set out to rape the young child but claimed that he'd raped her while he was intoxicated and that he'd killed her sort-of accidentally while he was frantically trying to get her to shut up. Although a cynic might have questioned Bill's explanation for why he had killed the girl, the imposition of a life sentence for second- rather than first- degree murder indicated that the court hadn't believed that, at least beyond a reasonable doubt, the killing had been premeditated.

And so, now having wormed – sorry, worked – his way from maximum to minimum security, Bill the Bricklayer's next quest was to gain some sort of release to the community, with full parole being his ultimate target. As a parolee with a life sentence, he would be required to report to a parole officer for the remainder of his days, but at least he'd be fairly free to roam about the community: good news for Bill, although perhaps not quite such glad tidings for the little girls out there.

Now well into his middle years and in a state of sobriety, Bill did not come across as the bug-eyed, drooling monster that his offense might have hinted at. At the same time, he wasn't a particularly likeable fellow and he didn't make the slightest effort to dazzle me with his charm or move beyond a basic level of grudging cooperation.

A heavy-set and slightly overweight guy with stringy, medium-length grey hair, he impressed me as being as a shrewd and self-assured fellow who'd been in the correctional system long enough to have become a solid con with the wherewithal to survive and make the most of his circumstances.

One of the many interesting things about Bill was that despite his participation in a variety of sex offender and other rehabilitative programs, he hadn't undergone any sort of sexual interest testing. His claim that he'd raped a young child almost by drunken accident rather than by design – thereby refuting the notion that he was a pedophile with a primary interest in pre-pubescent children – had never been tested or indeed seriously challenged.

He'd wended his way through the rehab programs, and he'd worked himself down to a low security level. Now, I don't know about you, but the guys I know aren't in the habit of getting themselves loaded and going out and raping and killing little girls. The fact that Bill had done just such a thing, drunk or not, was a big red flag warning of something sinister in his psyche.

But Bill had managed to persuade the correctional program officials that the booze had caused or at least catalyzed his offense, that he was sorry about what he'd done, and that he wouldn't do it again. Well, okay, Bill, if you say so, fair enough!

My thoughts regarding Bill's canniness were reinforced by the fact that when it came time to score and interpret his personality test (solid and sophisticated tests being scored and initially interpreted by computer, I might add) his results came back as invalid.

Bill's answers on the test had been sufficiently random and/or contradictory to prompt the scoring program to hypothesize that he hadn't answered the questions in a candid or straightforward fashion, and that no reliable conclusions could be drawn from his pattern of responses.

When questioned about this, Bill claimed that because he hadn't been wearing his reading glasses while taking the test, he'd had difficulty reading the questions. The thing is, when I'd administered the test inventory to him, which he'd completed in an average length of time, he hadn't said anything about needing glasses or having difficulty reading without them.

If he'd needed them, he could have asked me for a spare pair or he could have taken a minute to return to his room to retrieve his own glasses. Also, I had surreptitiously observed him while he was taking the test, and he'd shown absolutely no problems.

My examination of the pattern of test results, in conjunction with Bill's overall presentation and account of himself, led me to conclude that it was highly likely that he was attempting to 'game the system' by passive-aggressively undermining the assessment. In my subsequent report on him I noted these conclusions and related that I was unable to recommend that he be released on any kind of advance release or parole.

At the time the authorities heeded my concerns and Bill remained in custody. However, I have no doubt that as soon as he was able to do so (usually after a year or so has elapsed) Bill re-applied for early release. And it's more likely than not that eventually he managed to secure some sort of work release to the community, followed by day parole and ultimately full parole.

After that?

Well, if he hasn't drunk himself into an early grave or landed himself in more hot water by accidentally-on-purpose encountering and harming another child, he walks among us. And our children.

If I were to put money on it, I'd say that it's entirely conceivable that Bill murdered the child neither reactively nor accidentally (that is, panicking and trying to quiet the girl after she began to cry out, as he'd claimed) but because he'd wanted to eliminate the only person who could identify him. It is quite possible that he'd intended to kill her all along, to avoid detection or even for the perverse pleasure and supreme control of doing so.

Or for both reasons. It's imaginable that Bill had killed the girl in conjunction with his rape of her, deriving sexual satisfaction from the act, and/or getting just a bit too carried away while he was caught up in the throes of his adrenaline and testosterone-fuelled lust. Perhaps (we only have his word for it) his thinking, emotions and actions were distorted and intensified by his inebriated state.

Whatever the true motive for his heinous behavior, Bill certainly wouldn't have been the first person to have accepted a plea bargain – pleading guilty to a lesser charge (in this case second-degree murder) in order to avoid the expense and trouble of a trial and the possibility, if found guilty, of being convicted of a more serious offense and receiving a far stiffer sentence. Indeed, such negotiations between defense and prosecutor are the norm rather than the exception.

But what was apparent to me about Bill was that even in middle age he remained wily and passively resistant. And let's step back and take a look at what he'd done: drunk or not, he'd abducted a little girl for his own sexual gratification, and then he'd raped her and beaten her to death with a brick. Let that sink in.

What does this say about Bill's underlying character and his capacity for extraordinarily malicious selfishness and homicidal violence? Or had he miraculously mellowed over the years – even being nagged by feelings of compunction and shame at what he had done –no longer being the same individual who'd raped and killed an innocent child? You decide. All I know is that based on his offense and his account of what he'd done and why he'd done it, I had very grave concerns about him, as well as doubts about the authenticity of his explanation of why he'd murdered a young child.

Which is what I'd attempted to communicate to the parole board, in as professional and balanced a manner as possible – always bearing in mind that every single word in a forensic psychological report may end up being read back to you in a court of law, sometimes many years later.

But as ever, I got paid only to give my opinion, not to be an advocate for one side or the other, however strongly I may or may not have felt about Bill's character and his horrific misdeeds.

Bye, Bye Baby

Paulo was an odd guy who had sailed across the mystical line that supposedly separates sanity from insanity. I say supposedly because despite what some may tell you, what's real and not real, sane and insane, tends to be a bit subjective: the best that we can do is to agree that if most of us can reach a consensus on what constitutes reality, and it works to keep us all chugging along with some sort of harmony and grounding, we can call it real.

But the physicists will tell you that time does not really exist as we know it, and that everything that is so very solid really is just amorphous energy. So, you never really know. That said, Paulo was nuts.

In his mid-thirties at the time of the crime, Paulo was a fully-fledged, got the tats, running-with-rats, drinking the Kool-Aid member of a high-profile criminal gang. Having acquired such dubious status, one day Paulo decided that it would be an excellent idea to kill his gang leader's 6-month-old baby boy.

Paulo had previous drug-related convictions, but nothing in his background came close to the first-degree murder charge that brought him to my attention. Briefly, in the period leading up to his murder of the child, Paulo had become acutely paranoid and had been ratcheting-up his alcohol use.

Increasingly consumed by his paranoid delusions, he had concluded that his gang boss was planning to have him set-up and killed. Flowing from this logic and his desire to get even with his boss, he had conceived the novel solution of killing his boss's child so that he (Paulo) would be put in jail, where he believed that he would be safe.

Now, if we go along with Paulo's reasoning that because your criminal bossman is conspiring to kill you, you should get yourself off to prison (an abode which by definition is overflowing with nefarious criminals, some of whom were quite likely to have had connections with Paulo's gang) so as to be safe, it seems equally sensible to believe that an ideal way of getting into prison would be to kill your boss's child.

Armed with this logic, Paulo had taken a length of cord, sat down beside the baby in the back seat of his (the baby's) mother's car, and wrapped the cord tightly around the baby's neck. As he was strangled, petechiae permeated the boy's eyes (according to the autopsy report), from which the lights of life were extinguished. Somewhat alarmed at this unforeseen occurrence, the boy's mother – that is, the gang leader's wife – had leapt from the car, grabbed the baby and started to scream; whereupon Paulo, who clearly was an 'in for a penny, in for a pound' kind of guy, had attempted to run her down with her own car.

If nothing else, Paulo must be admired for taking the concept of 'getting your boss's attention' to an entirely new level.

Although Paulo's stated motivation for his actions was to exact revenge against his boss and to seek the security and sanctity of jail, it might come as no surprise that I found Paulo to be just a bit irrational in his thinking – indeed, sufficiently wacky to being patently delusional.

At the risk of repeating myself, killing your gang leader's son, attempting to kill his wife, and then being detained in a correctional setting that brought him into close contact with a motley crew of criminals and gang members is not a course of action that's likely to endear you to the underwriter of your life insurance policy.

Paulo was a bit of a blend of the very hardened and the very deranged individual: a law breaker who could strangle a baby and try to run down the child's mother, who at the same time clearly was a couple of sandwiches short of a picnic.

In what turned out to be a personally memorable and interesting case, I assessed Paulo on behalf of his defense attorney, who requested my involvement to determine whether Paulo was sane, *compos mentis* and likewise firing on all cylinders.

The defense team was pursuing a verdict of not guilty on account of insanity/mental disorder, and with this in mind the lawyer had requested my evaluation and testimony as to Paulo's state of mind preceding and at the time of his offense.

The hearing was quite a high-profile event, with a variety of expert witnesses being brought in to trot out their credentials, bleat their opinions, and bill generously for services rendered. The details of the case being what they were, the trial also attracted extensive media coverage. Fame and infamy being very close relations.

In addition to the nature of the crime itself, one fascinating aspect about Paulo's case was that the defense team had access to the police interview/interrogation of their client, and I was asked to watch the video and opine on factors such as Paulo's state of mind during the interview, the techniques utiilized by the detectives, and whether or not Paulo's statement could be relied upon as being uncoerced and factual.

As I viewed the recording, it was clear from the outset of the interview that Paulo was not functioning well, and that he was highly stressed, distressed, and mentally disordered. Rather than using the best practice interviewing techniques often employed nowadays (and having seen the transcripts of a lot of police interviews, I've got a pretty good idea of how they work and are supposed to work – my unsolicited advice therefore being never to believe that the interviewing police officer is your friend and never to give a statement to the police unless specifically advised to do so by your lawyer), the detectives appeared to have taken advantage of Paulo's intense anguish and mental confusion in order to extract a confession.

Of course, given that it had been Paulo's intention to commit a murder so that he could go to jail, even if the detectives had done and said nothing his confession may well have been easy to extract.

So, Paulo's confession certainly did not mean that he hadn't committed the crime, because he had. But it did lend credence to the defense's position that he was exhibiting signs of mental malaise around the time that he'd perpetrated the murder, which in turn also suggested that he was likely to have been mentally disturbed during the criminal act itself. It also undermined the prosecution's slam-dunk case, which was predicated primarily on Paulo's police confession.

Despite the fact that by the time Paulo's case came my way I'd already provided testimony at various levels of court, including the supreme or superior court, this trial was a big deal: there had been a murder; there was major criminal gang involvement, the victim was the gang leader's baby, the alleged murderer was a gang member, and the accused was pursuing a not-guilty-due-to-insanity defense.

Especially with the attention paid to it by the media, the stakes obviously were high. And the pressure was ratcheted up a notch when I sat down for dinner with my immediate and extended family one fine Sunday evening, only to hear the fax machine ringing in my home office. I never did learn how to separate work from home, workweek from weekend, or practise any of those other psychologically healthy workplace techniques that we mental health types preach, and on evenings and weekends I would forward my phone and fax lines from my office to my home.

After dinner, I padded wearily and warily into my home office, in a state of postprandial torpor. Suddenly alert, my heart skipped and quickened at the sight of a plethora of pages, conveyed electronically to me by Paulo's lawyer, in which the attorney had kindly listed all the questions he intended to ask me during direct examination in court.

Fine.

But what galled me was that the lawyer also had written in full all my responses to his questions! Such preparation of the witness, as it is euphemistically called, certainly is not unusual. And perhaps it's just me, but I consider it to be, well, rather presumptuous and professionally undignified for the lawyer to furnish both the questions *and* the expected answers for direct examination.

Now, although some may think otherwise, my job as a retained expert witness, was to objectively communicate my professional findings and opinions to the court. At least theoretically (there have been many hired guns, and there will be many more), I was not being retained to function as a spokesperson for the lawyer, an advocate for his client, or a purveyor of the opinion that the lawyer wanted.

But because attorneys are paid to represent and advocate for their clients, a lot of defense lawyers find it difficult to understand and accept the fact that their retained experts aren't also going to advocate for their position. And this lawyer, who was an aggressive and well-known counselor, was one of those.

Well, the fateful day arrived, and I appeared at the fancy supreme courthouse and dutifully hung around the designated courtroom for a couple of hours, waiting for my name to be called. When I was summoned, I obediently strode into the courtroom and, with my usual air of (ersatz) assuredness, assumed my position in the witness box.

As an aside, it was my policy to peer through the wee window in the courtroom door before being called, to familiarize myself with the layout of the room and thus to be able to march confidently to the witness box, as if I knew what I was doing. Having found my way there in this case, I was sworn in and launched into my testimony.

From my perspective, my oral testimony went well enough, and there were no big surprises. The lead defense attorney asked his scripted questions very much as they had been disgorged from my fax machine a few nights earlier. The lawyer had the advantage of being able to read his questions, and I fully expect that he also had my expected responses typed neatly beneath his points of inquiry.

For my part, I certainly hadn't memorized his recommended answers, and the attorney didn't get all of the replies he'd anticipated: at one point I responded in a completely different way than he'd expected, obviously unsettling him a little. But at the end of the day, on my own terms and in my own words, I communicated my opinion to the court, and in fact my views were likely to have been helpful to Paulo's case.

A memorable moment in my testimony did come during cross-examination, however, when the lead prosecutor asked me a hypothetical question which simply could not be answered with a yes or no, as he was demanding. As is customary in such instances, I turned to the judge and advised him of my inability to respond categorically to the question, without qualification and explanation. The judge irascibly and irrationally (I was later informed that he was a civil trial judge, and that he was out of his depth in a criminal trial, especially one of such magnitude) directed me to answer yes or no.

Such is the erudition and impartiality of the judiciary. The pompous oaf (and I mean that in the nicest possible way). Nonetheless, at the conclusion of the trial my opinion that Paulo was psychotic and therefore not criminally responsible for his actions when he murdered the child, was the verdict of the court.

Accordingly, Paulo was transferred back to the psychiatric hospital at which he'd previously spent time. And there he would remain until he was deemed to be sane and no longer a threat to society. Or in Paulo's case, given his shaky immigration status, until he could attend an immigration hearing that undoubtedly would result in an order for him to be deported to his country of origin.

Given the fact that the gang to which he had formerly belonged had extensive connections in that country, Paulo's prospects for a happy and healthy extended lifespan were not looking good. I would imagine that by now, a couple of decades on, he's either dead or, languishing inside a high-security, long-term psychiatric ward, wishing that he were.

A Family Affair

At the opposite end of the spectrum from the murder committed by poor Paulo was one that was perpetrated by a couple of young guys by the name of Jay and Brad. Murders, to be more precise. Brad and Jay had eliminated three people, all of whom had been members of the same family.

The two handsome and well-coiffed dudes were in their early twenties when I first met them, very shortly after their admission to a pre-trial detention center. They were close friends (as well as a mutual admiration and supportive duo) and neither of them had a prior criminal history.

At the time, Brad and Jay stood accused of murdering Brad's parents and sibling. The family had been brutally bludgeoned to death. The crime scene, which was Brad's upscale family home, was bathed in blood and bits of brain matter, and there were no survivors. The alleged motivation was the expedient and perennial one of financial gain.

An insurance policy had been taken out on Brad's parents and as the sole survivor Brad stood to be the beneficiary of that as well as the inheritor of the family home and other material assets.

Although I didn't conduct a formal assessment of either Jay or Brad, I did get to interview both of them upon several occasions and got a good take on their personalities. What impressed me the most about them was their composed and very self-assured (some might even say smug) presentation.

They came across as a couple of young guys who'd grown up with feelings of entitlement. In Brad's case, he was relaxed and nonchalant to the point of interjecting humor into our conversation, which you'll recall had first occurred very shortly after the sudden and savage murder of several members of his immediate family. If nothing else, some semblance of sorrow and shock, or at the very least expressions of sober remorse, might have lent support to his claims of innocence.

Without saying so, both conveyed to me their supreme belief that they'd be exonerated on their charges and that their current detention was merely an inconvenience – and I'm sure something for them to brag about later.

Classification policy at the remand center stipulated that all co-accused were to be housed on separate living units, so Jay and Brad were kept apart. Their stay at the center was unremarkable, save for the fact that Jay managed to get himself beaten up quite badly. His face was seriously contused and swollen, and his ego was similarly bruised, when I saw him after that incident, at which point he wasn't his usual insouciant self, and he clearly failed to see any humor in the situation.

It was my impression that Jay's tendency to come across with a certain superior air of privilege and arrogance, with corresponding disdain if not disrespect for others, had had something to do with the assault.

Following their trial, Jay and Brad were convicted of the first-degree murders of Brad's family and were given life sentences. Reportedly, Jay was the one who'd actually wielded the baseball bat with which he'd systematically beaten to death Brad's parents and sibling, with Brad acting as his very willing and motivated accomplice.

Subsequent reports indicate that as the years unfolded and their hopes of a successful appeal or other miraculous liberation faded, Brad and Jay's swagger had sagged, and the psychopathic, egocentric and similar characteristics that had helped them to feel detached and calm when they'd entered prison, had failed to protect them from the debilitating hardships of long-term incarceration.

A murder of expedience that, apart from the lawyers, turned out to have been unbeneficial to everyone concerned. The result: a dead family and two young men whose lives began to shrivel and die the moment they were arrested.

What a waste. Greed coupled with youthful ignorance and arrogance had won the day, while Brad and Jay had lost everything of value in their lives and Brad's family had quite literally lost their lives.

Interrogation I

The aloof callousness shown by Brad and Jay, and their use of murder as an expedient tool, also were present in the case 'Brillo' Brian. (For those unfamiliar with the Brillo pad, it's a small pad made of steel wool that's been impregnated with soap; it's used when washing dishes to scour out particularly grubby pans. They're great.) Although Brian was doing time for second degree murder, his offence was first-class.

At the time of our encounter, Brian was a resident of a medium-security correctional institution. In his late thirties and still sporting dark brown hair, he was one of those solid, hardened cons who carried themselves with the pragmatic, no-nonsense, don't-mess-with-me demeanor that tends to work well in prisons. He was the sort of guy with whom someone such as me could establish a basic functional relationship, sufficient to complete a forensic psychological evaluation for instance, but characterized neither by bonhomie nor genuine rapport.

Beers with Brian would not be high on my bucket list.

Brian's index offense – that is, the one for which he was serving his current sentence, and which had brought him to my attention – was the murder of another denizen of the criminal underworld. The information on file (Brian being tight-lipped about the entire affair, I had to rely solely on the official account) indicated that he had been directed by his criminal superiors to interrogate a member of a rival faction, and that following their fireside chat he had dispatched the individual in question to that great parlor in the sky.

Brian had accomplished this task with diligence, by securing his victim to a chair and then applying various crude but effective methods with which to encourage his guest to disclose information. Brillo pads had featured prominently in Bill's endeavors – hence the nickname that I've attached to him. I would imagine that steel wool or its equivalent can make quite an impression on bare skin, and in the reports on file the insertion of the pads into the victim's mouth and other parts of his anatomy also was mentioned, together with a sustained and more generalized pummeling. Such innovation!

Although I assume that Brian had paused his torturous activities long enough for some personal rest and relaxation, he'd managed to keep it up for a number of days, at the end of which he had checked his debrided guest out of this vale of tears.

Given his demonstrated capacity to partake in such behavior, it came as no surprise that Brian came across as he did. In fact, had he tried to present as a pleasant and engaging guy I would have smelled a rat and suspected either that his psychopathy was showing and that he was attempting to charm and con me.

As it turned out, Brian didn't try to appeal to my good nature or persuade me that he'd been unjustly judged – he just went through the motions of the assessment and met the basic requirements of speaking with me and completing testing. For Brian, it was all part of the job and the game.

To his credit, Brian was true to himself, and he didn't pretend to be anyone other than the hardboiled individual that he was. His clinical presentation was confirmed by a psychological profile that showed no mental disorder, average intelligence, and an antisocial personality.

He was the kind of guy who doesn't have too much difficulty serving his sentence – he could take care of himself physically, his offense would have conveyed a certain amount of respect and fear, and it's highly likely that he had pre-established connections within the inmate population. I expect that over time he'd managed to work the system as best he could so as to endure his incarceration, slog his way toward a parole hearing and eventually rejoin his criminal companions in the community.

And of course, that is the reality for guys like Brian: eventually nearly all of those who enter the joint emerge from behind the steely gates and stroll among us once again. Something to consider when we baulk at the efforts that may be undertaken to rehabilitate, or at least to make no worse, the people we incarcerate.

Unless we genuinely want to lock up most offenders for the entirety of their lives (which if nothing else would be exorbitantly and prohibitively expensive for the taxpayer), our prisons are simply housing these guys for a bit, then depositing them back in the community. So, even from a position of self-interest, it befits us to try to ensure that Brian and his ilk don't come out quite as bad – or at a minimum no more violent, hard, and filled with cold anger – than they were when they went in.

Or, to make very sure that we do our absolute best to ensure that we don't cross their paths after their release.

I saw Carl at the request of his defense attorney (who later went on to become a prosecutor and then a judge), who was quite interested in finessing her client into the most lenient sentence into which he could fit. After some bargaining, Carl had ended up pleading guilty to manslaughter. There were not a lot of mitigating circumstances, given the calculated nature of the offense and the presence of a very tangible *corpus delicti*.

As always in such cases, my goal as a hopefully and ideally unbiased assessor was to conduct an objective psychological evaluation and to report my findings to the lawyer. It was then up to that defense attorney to decide what they wanted to do with the report. Which meant that the report was not automatically released to the prosecution and the court. In a vast majority of defense cases in which I've been involved the referring attorney used my reports, and thus they became part of the judicial process by being submitted into evidence.

However, I've no doubt that periodically defense attorneys have considered my observations and opinions to have been unhelpful to their client, whereupon my report would have been quietly but unceremoniously ditched. This didn't bother me in the slightest (really – well, perhaps a slim slight...), provided that payment for services was rendered within 30 days.

Carl's killing bore some similarities to Brian's, in that the murder had been an expedient one, the by-product of a turf war between rival criminal factions. Also, the victim had been subjected to physical abuse (torture) prior to being killed – as with Brian, probably to extract information and to convey a message to the opposing criminal gang.

For some reason, in this case the collateral documentation provided to me by the lawyer contained a very charming collection of color photographs of the male victim, who (as often seems to be the case once they pass over the finish line – getting there is the tough part) appeared to be quite composed, nonchalant, and even slightly amused, postmortem.

Death, I guess, does have its benefits. Anyway, notable was the fact that the guy's face and trunk sported multiple cigarette burns, undoubtedly administered not by a careless or inebriated smoker but by someone who was intent on methodically and pragmatically inflicting smouldering pain on the poor guy.

As memory serves, the victim's final inability to suck air had been attributable to the insertion of a knife into his bared upper torso, as well as constriction of his throat by a pair of hands held tightly around it.

All of which once again really raises the point that there are indeed different strokes for different folks, and that not everyone thinks, feels, acts or in fact is the same. There are some people who simply have little or no regard for the life or well-being of others and have few or no qualms about maliciously hurting and killing humans and animals.

Such individuals view other beings as objects or things, rather than sentient creatures, and have little or no capacity to empathize with that being. These people can't stick even a toe into another person's moccasins, let alone walk in them. It can be extraordinarily difficult – some may say impossible – to get such a person to develop true sensitivity for any being other than themselves, although psychopathy often dissipates or burns-off at bit as we age and experience what's known as psychopathic burn-out.

Growing old is not, as they say, for the faint of heart, not even for the psychopath.

Speaking of animals, cruelty to animals during childhood is a surprisingly good harbinger of major problems of adjustment and behavior in adulthood: those who enjoy abusing and killing animals while they're still wee urchins are likely to have some seriously messed-up background and personality factors that are unlikely to improve as they grow older.

Although we rely on tough individuals, such as soldiers who are inured to fighting and death, to keep us safe on our sofas and smugly liberal in our politics, when it comes to those who have absolutely no compunction about taking life, or even enjoy the process of doing so, we're usually dealing with a psychopathic and sometimes sadistic soul.

That said, I didn't find Carl to be such a person. Sure, he was a fairly burly boy (actually in his forties, but most of those types of guys are forever in their mid-to-late teens in terms of their emotional development – which interestingly enough just happens to be quite a psychopathic stage of life for many of us), a Caucasian with medium length greying hair, who looked as though he could handle himself well in a bar fight, but who didn't come across as particularly callous or conning.

As we talked about his offense, he gave the impression that he'd had a job to do, that he hadn't particularly enjoyed doing it, and that the death of his victim had been neither intended nor desired. If that were to be the case, the choking must have been inadvertently continued for a touch too long – I suppose that in the midst of a good interrogation and torture one can lose all track of time and tightness!

Be that as it may, psych testing revealed nothing particularly remarkable about Carl except for the fact that, to no one's surprise, his interests were more on the masculine, mechanical and practical side of things than on the artistic or aesthetic: you were less likely to find Carl musing about the merits of Bach over Beethoven or Gauguin over Van Gogh, than you were to find him tinkering with the old jalopy.

I reported as much to Carl's attorney, alongside my opinion that I had found nothing psychologically notable or homicidal about her client, other than the fact that he'd killed someone after methodically abusing him.

When the day came, Carl was sentenced for the lesser charge of manslaughter as opposed to murder, and to the relief of both Carl and his lawyer he was awarded the modest sentence of eleven years of imprisonment. Not too harsh a penalty to pay for having slowly and cruelly taken someone else's life.

Barring re-offense, Carl would be a free man by now. A bit long in the tooth, but potentially still in the enforcement and interrogation business. I wonder whether he's quit smoking – or at least learned to be a bit more careful where he puts his glowing cigarette tips.

My guess is that the answer to both questions is no, but we can always hope for psychopathic burn-out.

Her Spirit Soared

As a counterpoint to the cold-blooded and expedient nature of Carl's, Brad's, Jay's and Brian's offenses, we now move on to a murder in which the passions of power, sex, lust, and rage figured prominently: emotions without which the forensic psychologist would be bored and bankrupt!

The kind of killing that's typically committed by an individual who derives pleasure, or at least a sense of perverse satisfaction, from taking another person's life. Such pleasure usually is sexual in nature and is tightly connected with the feelings of extreme dominance and control that can be affiliated with the act of murder.

There are differences in the degree of emotionality surrounding the killing – ranging from the guy who bites and tears in the frenzied throes of sexual lust, to the individual who rapes, strangles, and then methodically mutilates his victim. But the commonality is that in this kind of case the overall act of killing is fraught with significantly heightened emotionality and sexual arousal.

I know of women who have derived sexual satisfaction from killing – one female serial killer bragging that she experienced an orgasm every time she took someone's life, which she'd accomplished by stabbing – but I've never had the opportunity to meet such a woman in person – at least, not that I know of, and at least not professionally.

In contrast, I have met a number of men who have killed during or after their sexual assault of the victim.

One such fellow was Chris, the guy I mentioned briefly at the beginning of this book who had taken the life of a woman by stabbing her in the chest. Chris was a mustachioed fellow in his late twenties or early thirties at the time, with dark brown hair and, one may speculate, a dark brown or black soul. I met with him on several occasions at the pretrial center while he was awaiting trial.

As with many others at the center, I saw Chris primarily for monitoring purposes, to forestall any major deterioration in his mental state. Such contact was particularly warranted in his case because he had borderline aspects to his personality.

This meant that he wasn't sufficiently mentally disordered to be diagnosed as such, but neither was he entirely stable or normal – one of those somewhat odd and often difficult people who frequently present with weird obsessions and extremes of emotion. And as Chris' crime exemplified, he was not weird in a good way.

I had some interesting and at times extended conversations with Chris. While he was in the pretrial facility, he didn't go any further downhill from where he was usually at mentally – at least not a long way down – and I like to think that my therapeutic conversations with him helped to stabilize him. He ended up pleading guilty to murder.

But enroute to that guilty plea, and despite my admonitions for him not to talk about his alleged offense, Chris clearly felt the need to share with me the details of what he obviously believed was an important and even spiritually uplifting experience.

As related to me by Chris, after he had abducted and raped his young adult female victim, he'd taken her life by stabbing her with a knife. And as he spoke, I gained the impression that the stabbing had been entirely premeditated, in that the killing had been a part of his modus operandi, providing him with pleasure or at least the satiation of his lustful and hateful drives.

Sad to say that in the dark forensic world there was nothing particularly unusual or odd about that, despite the heinous nature of the homicide and the path that had led to that homicide. The really strange thing about this case was that as he'd plunged the knife into the woman's chest, Chris had seen her soul leave her body and rise upwards.

I can still see him in my mind's eye as he shared this revelation with me, sitting hunched over in his prison coveralls, speaking in hushed and reverential tones. Even in comparison with some of the bizarre chats that I've had with offenders, this conversation had indeed taken a mystically murky and otherworldly weird turn.

For Chris, this had been a momentous, memorable, and even moving experience for him, and it was fascinating to hear him speak of it and to see how it had affected him. This was not one of your everyday, run-of-the-mill rape-and-murder-of-a-stranger-cases. This man had had something akin to a religious experience after he'd plunged in the knife between his victim's breasts.

Alas, it seems to me that the 'soul' arising from the woman's dying body had not been ectoplasm but vapor – vapor as steam that had been generated by the warm, moist air from her lungs meeting the cooler ambient air.

However, I didn't communicate this much more mundane explanation to Chris – in part because I thought that his belief that he'd seen her soul might, in some unknown way, bolster his capacity to experience feelings of compunction concerning his extraordinarily selfish crime and the absolute horror that it had wrought. I also didn't want to undermine a belief that obviously was very important to him and which in a convoluted sort of way seemed to be helping him to retain a grasp on everyday reality.

I wonder whether Chris still believes that he saw his victim's soul moving heavenward. Or if he even cares. And if does still believe, how does this make him feel as he reflects upon the event in his cell, counting out the decades of his prison term and counting down toward his own soul's ascent – or descent – as it leaves his body.

Regardless of whether Chris continues to believe in soul-spotting, my conversations with him had signified that his motivation for murder lay in his fundamental desire to experience the sensation of killing a woman, which in turn had been strongly associated with the sexual satiation and power dynamics of his offending behavior as well as his hatred of women.

Principally, his was a lust murder, coupled as it was with the sexual arousal and satisfaction he had derived from dominating, raping, and killing his victim. Although more practical considerations associated with the need to eliminate the one witness who could have identified him also may have been in the back of Chris' mind, at heart it flowed from the dark, broiling, and (at least for most sane people) unfathomable emotions and drives which percolated within him. And of course, let's not forget that not only had Chris entertained those thoughts and impulses – he'd acted upon them.

Chris had raped and killed someone merely to satisfy his desires. And it can only be hoped that in the unlikely event that he ever be allowed to step outside the prison walls one day, his 'spiritual' experience would serve as a deterrent and disincentive to his perpetration of additional homicidal horrors.

We can only pray that his mind remains haunted by the rising soul of the young woman whose life he so capriciously and viciously terminated.

Bitten by Love

Reminiscing about Chris the Soul Spotter makes me think of Glen, a fellow who was in his mid-forties and an inmate at a medium-security federal correctional institution at the time our paths crossed. Glen was into his fifteenth year of a life sentence that had been imposed for his murder of a young woman.

Although he'd come into contact with the criminal justice system prior to his current offense, his past misconduct had been relatively trivial in nature (as are most things, relative to murder) and apparently his prior bad behavior had given no forewarning of the homicidal horrors that had culminated in his current detention.

Even by this forensic psychologist's standards, Glen's index offense had been a particularly brutal and bloody one. Glen had raped his victim, who had been a casual acquaintance of his. Reports indicated that before, during, or after his penetration of her, he had strangled her. Indeed, strangulation was given as the official cause of death. But before killing the woman (I say before, but this is a bit of a presumption – as you may have gathered there is a diversity of tastes, and post-mortem cannibalism is not out of the question), Glen had bitten off one of her nipples.

He had also used his teeth to tear out a portion of her genitalia. Her mutilated body was found in a semi-secluded area not too far from his residence, and it didn't take long for Glen to be arrested, charged and convicted of her murder.

Glen had done very well in custody. He'd participated in high-intensity sex offender treatment programs and had been transferred from a maximum- to a medium-security prison. Program and clinical staff alike had expressed their generally positive feelings about Glen's progress.

His smiling visage even had been published in a local newspaper – a portrayal of a model prisoner who was involved in some sort of arts project which supposedly exemplified inmate good works and rehabilitation. The prevailing motivational/etiological theory for his crime, likely based at least initially on Glen's account of how his offense had unfolded, was that his victim had spurned his advances, in response to which he'd taken umbrage, and in an enraged state he'd forced himself on her, committed the other identified acts of aggression, and sort of accidentally killed her.

After some time, Glen was deemed to have addressed relevant offending issues, to be at reduced risk, and therefore able to move forward with his life. Which of course was much more than could be said for his victim.

As an external consultant to the prison at which Glen was based, I was asked to evaluate him to check where he was at psychologically and to verify that, as almost everyone seemed to be saying, he was at low risk to reoffend and potentially a good candidate for some sort of graduated reintegration into the community.

The thing was, when I looked at Glen's file the alarm bells began to ring loudly in my head: there was something that wasn't quite right. And my concerns were heightened following my subsequent interview and testing of Glen. Call me naïve or call me cynical (I blushingly confess to being both), but it certainly appeared to me that, despite all of the programs he'd taken, neither he nor the program staff had truly investigated, accepted, or dealt meaningfully with the factors that had really motivated his offense.

Now, I don't know about you, but the last time I got turned down for a date I think that my feelings and pride may have been a bit hurt, and my self-confidence a little wounded, but I don't recall having slipped into a homicidal, enraged sexual attack on the object of my amorous desires.

The mutilation and murder of the victim, purportedly ensuing from her spurning of Glen's advances, were highly suggestive of his sexual frenzy during his offense, in the throes of which he'd bitten into his victim, tearing off parts of her body.

Moreover, his buccal removal of symbols of the woman's femininity – namely, one of her nipples and some of her labial tissue – implied something else: without delving too deeply into the mysterious realms of Freudian theory, I was getting strong vibes about the presence of some seriously hostile attitudes toward women. Such possibilities evidently hadn't even been touched upon, let alone meaningfully addressed, during Glen's treatment, and if left unaddressed they dramatically increased his risk for some very nasty future behavioural difficulties.

Much to Glen's chagrin, I communicated this opinion to the correctional and treatment team, with the strong recommendation that he should receive additional, focused intervention to target the factors underlying his extremely serious offense.

I have no way of knowing what happened to him over the longer term, but I do know that at the very least his plans to facilitate and expedite his release from custody were delayed until such time that he and his treatment team had re-assessed his rehabilitative plan and addressed all relevant risk factors. To be honest, given the dynamics of his offense, just keeping Glen in custody until he'd had more time to 'mature' (a euphemism for getting sufficiently old and sexually diminished that his risk would naturally decline) would be likely to enhance the safety of the females in the community.

Frankly, I'm not optimistic that treatment alone would do a great deal to reduce recidivistic risk in a case like Glen's – although probably it wouldn't hurt, and it might even be of some help. Sadly, the true risk reducer would be time and an associated diminution of Glen's testosterone, sexual desire, energy, and general physical capacity. Glen requiring a wheelchair or a walker to get around would be an outstanding risk reduction strategy.

The Sick Stick Man

No one had even tried to get Leroy to participate in the treatment and other programs that Glen had enjoyed. When I encountered him, Leroy was a stringy-haired guy in his early twenties who was doing life for first degree murder. His victim was a 16-year-old girl who had been beaten and choked to death. Oh yes, she'd also had sticks inserted into her vagina and rectum.

For good measure, post-mortem examination revealed that a stick had been pushed into one of the girl's eye sockets, and that (shades of Glen) the girl had been bitten on an arm and one of her breasts. The reports on file indicated that Leroy had responded badly to the girl's rejection of his affectionate overtures.

Rather than going home and sulking and smoking weed, he'd taken a more direct and sinister approach. Clearly, like Glen, Leroy was a sensitive soul who had a tough time handling rejection.

After the murder and additional violation of the teenaged girl, Leroy had been sufficiently moved by events that he'd returned to the crime scene to retrieve a souvenir. Later, he'd also attended his victim's funeral, where he and a companion were seen laughing. In subsequent discussion with an undercover police officer, Leroy was said to have admitted to the murder of the girl, and to have described to the officer how he'd jammed the sticks into her body.

Reading about the offense and associated particulars in Leroy's clinical file provided me with a preliminary impression of the possible psychological forces at play and what sort of a guy I'd be dealing with.

However, by the time I met with him, Leroy had been in maximum-security custody for over three years and was destined to remain incarcerated for many more years. By that point, he was neither laughing nor smiling, and neither was he acknowledging his culpability for his offense.

Underscoring the necessity for professional psychologists, and especially forensic examiners, to set aside their prejudices and preconceived notions, the purpose for my assessment of Leroy pertained to his request to have private family visits. His quest for such visits having been connected with his stated plans to marry his girlfriend. So, a few years after being convicted of a particularly vicious and sadistic murder, young Leroy was intending to move on with his life by getting married – or at least, with professed matrimonial intentions, looking forward to enjoying a little prenuptial nooky in the conjugal visitation quarters.

You must give Leroy a certain amount of grudging admiration for his capacity to compartmentalize, move forward, and use the system for maximum personal gain.

Considering such aspirations, you might have thought that Leroy would have been keen to make as favorable an impression on me as possible, and to at least talk the good talk during the clinical interview. Or at the very least, not to make me angry.

However, when I spoke with him, he proved to be a truculent guy who clearly was unimpressed by my social charms. He denied having been responsible for the murder. He was quite terse in his answers, and he was reluctant to divulge personal information. He also proved to be extremely wary of the main psychological test that was administered to him: so much so, in fact, that his test results were invalidated by his double marking of some test items and his failure to respond to several other questions.

Leroy found it difficult to mask his underlying antisociality – even when it would have been very much in his best interests to do so. Although he was not without intelligence, he showed little insight into himself. Indeed, even though the psychological evaluation was necessary for him to proceed with his conjugal visit, he was highly resistant to the assessment. With some offenders, particularly those who have been in the correctional system for a while and have undergone a number of psych evaluations, such defensiveness may have been intensified by previously unfavorable psychological reports about them.

Regarding this, it's been my experience that some offenders have a generous capacity to see themselves in a positive light – or at least to project the blame for their own faults and misdeeds onto others – and when mental health clinicians have the audacity to suggest that they may be less than perfect, they're quick to blame the shrinks rather than themselves.

However, I was the first psychologist to have examined Leroy, so his distrust came not from negative experiences with prior forensic reports but from a more abiding and characterological resistance to authority and to any perceived loss of control. Given the nature of his offense, and his ongoing denial, a major reluctance to have his darker impulses and inclinations exposed to the light of day also may have contributed to his resistance.

Even sadistic sexual murderers can be shy, I suppose.

I don't know whether Leroy ever was allowed to have his private family visits or whether he went on to get married and live happily ever after. I do know that as far as I could determine, such ambitions, especially so early in his sentence, revealed his overall attitude toward his offense and his circumstances.

The referral by the correctional authorities also was extremely interesting and unusual, given the early stage of his life sentence, the dynamics of his offense, his continued denial, and his lack of participation in any rehabilitative programs.

Despite the fact that the courts at least theoretically maintain a presumption of innocence until the evidence indicates otherwise (even though by the law of averages and human fallibilities a small percentage of the offenders I've seen really would have been innocent), after a finding of guilt the forensic examiner must presume that the person really is guilty.

This was especially true in Leroy's case, in which there was surveillance and other tangible evidence. As I saw it, barring some sort of epiphany on Leroy's part, any efforts to "rehabilitate" him would be extremely challenging. For one thing, you'd have to overcome his denial – usually this would occur only after he'd participated in required treatment programs, exhausted all avenues of appeal, and grudgingly come to the realization that it would be in his own best interests (self-reference being something that I've found to be a central characteristic of most criminals) to fess up.

Even with such an admission of culpability, and his acknowledgement that he had issues that needed to be addressed, the road to Leroy's healing would be a long, rocky, and probably barren one. Although substance use may or may not have been a contributing factor, the dynamics of Leroy's offense and his subsequent actions denoted both serious pathology and psychopathy.

As with Glen, elements of sexual frenzy and genuine homicidal-level misogyny appear to have been present. In addition, to put it mildly, an intolerance to frustration and a major deficiency of anger management skills would appear to have been causally involved.

How do we cure such ailments?

Well, the reality is that we don't. We just do the best that we can to enable the offender to gain a better understanding of what motivated or fuelled their offending behavior and to manage their impulses and risk factors more effectively.

But as discussed earlier, in most such cases it's Father Time who is the most effective risk management agent: biological aging and burn-out being the elements which truly enable guys like Leroy and Glen to sit in the parks and stroll on the sidewalks beside us. And in some cases, as much as some academics and clinicians would like to believe otherwise, such salutary maturation never is attained, and the individual remains at risk until he is sufficiently disinterested and physically incapable of posing much of a threat to anyone.

At the time of writing Leroy has spent about half of his life in a correctional institution, and I hope that, like fine wine, he is aging well and will continue to do so until fully matured – or corked.

Until Death Do Us Part

In the interests of gender equality, equity and/or diversity, let's discuss one of the females I've assessed. Gloria was a previously law-abiding and ostensibly strait-laced woman in her early forties when she came to my attention – my services having been requested by her defense attorney, who wanted to know a bit more about what made Gloria tick and in particular how to use such knowledge to his and Gloria's advantage during sentencing negotiations.

Gloria was not a murderer or attempted murderer, but she was the next best thing, awaiting sentencing on a charge of conspiracy to commit the murder of her nearly dearly departed husband. Conspiracy to murder is such a profoundly serious criminal offense that, at least in principle, it can carry a penalty as severe as an actual homicide.

The reality however is that very few women who engage in such conspiracy or counseling to commit murder – and over the years there do seem to have been a fair number – receive sentences that are anywhere near those given to the people who plan and commit the murders. In fact, females almost always receive sentences that are more lenient than those meted out to their male counterparts – but that's a discussion for another day.

Gloria was quite a diminutive and softly spoken woman. She was mousey, certainly no enchanter, and didn't come across as someone who was capable of homicide or even quaffing a seriously strong cup of tea. As noted, she'd had no previous involvement with the criminal justice system and hitherto had led quite an ordinary life. Married for about 15 years, with no children. But appearances and histories can be deceptive.

My assessment of Gloria revealed no evidence of a mental disorder. She wasn't clinically depressed or anxious – although naturally, given her legal circumstances, she wasn't especially happy either, and in fact she was understandably tense and worried about her situation.

What lingers in my mind about Gloria is the fact that: a) her collaboration with her would-be spousal assassin actually had been with an undercover police officer, so presumably someone had tipped-off the authorities about her quest to recruit the services of a murderer-for-hire; and b) I was unable to establish a clear motive for why she had wanted to have her husband killed. There had to be a motive, of course – it's just that I couldn't get Gloria to talk to me about it.

Who knows, maybe she didn't even know her motivation, at least not consciously. Based on her actions and statements it would be fair to note that she didn't care deeply for her spouse, but neither did she express any great loathing of him. She didn't claim that he had been abusive, unfaithful, odious or malodorous. He didn't even hog the tv remote.

Digging a little deeper, although there was no obvious financial gain, presumably in the event of her spouse's demise Gloria would have stood to gain sole ownership of all his assets as well as their mutual property, probably alongside a nice insurance payout. So, money and a loveless marriage – and perhaps ennui, and for all I know an exciting younger lover – were about the best motivators that I could identify or speculate about. Not great motivations or exculpatory reasons to benefit or excite the defense attorney.

But how does someone go from "loving" and marrying another individual to not caring for them to such a degree that you are willing to go out and recruit someone to terminate their life? The marriage vows do say something about 'til death do us part, and Billy the Bard had something to say about the course of true love never running smoothly, but murdering a mate is taking things a wee bit too far, I think.

It would indeed appear to take a special kind of person to engage in such behavior, and without a compelling motivation such as desperation to avoid continued harm to oneself or one's loved ones, what could inspire a person to do such a thing, and what type of person would commit such a calculated and cold-blooded deed?

Well, the answer to the first part of the question is likely to revolve around a dysfunctional, loveless and/or unstimulating relationship, often in conjunction with avarice and expedience: in short, a desire to be unencumbered and affluent.

The answer to the second part of the question likely involves our old pals selfishness, shallow self-reference and, at its extreme, psychopathy. Someone who is sufficiently egocentric, unempathetic, callous, and cunning that they are willing to murder their partner, if only by proxy.

Well, it must be said that Gloria didn't come across as someone who was readily identifiable as a psychopath, but then the psychopathy checklist was based on males, and female psychopaths have been the subject of far less research than their male counterparts.

We tend to want to believe that females are softer, gentler, kinder, and more caring than males, but such is not always the case. Indeed, females can be every bit as ruthless as males, but may exhibit such ruthlessness in more subtle and oblique ways.

Gloria was notably unemotional about her offense, and her low mood and tension were at least primarily a side effect of her legal situation rather than attributable to any angst and gnashing of teeth over the error of her ways. So, there were hints of significant self-reference alongside a few psychopathic features.

But all that I was able to meaningfully and reliably convey to Gloria's lawyer was that she (Gloria, not the lawyer – although I have known a few unbalanced and psychopathic attorneys) wasn't mentally ill or generally antisocial, that she wasn't likely to be someone who was impulsive or inclined to engage in gratuitous or impetuous acts of aggression, and that she was expressing feelings of regret about having tried to hire someone to kill her husband. Or at least regret about having been caught trying to hire someone to knock off hubby. Her risk for general or violent recidivism was judged to be low.

Not much meat on the explanatory bone but enough to give her attorney and the court sufficient information with which to understand her basic psychological and behavioral profile, and from that to determine the likelihood of any type of re-offense.

Because there were no aggravating circumstances (not that conspiring to have your husband killed isn't aggravating enough, particularly if you're the husband) and the spouse wasn't actually killed, Gloria received a relatively minor sentence for her troubles, in the form of a short term of incarceration followed by a period of community supervision.

I don't know what happened to her after that. I expect that she would have behaved very well in a minimum-security female prison and likely would have been released early from custody. By now she may be happily remarried to some lucky guy, living the dream in an average, middle-class home and holding average, middle-class aspirations to pay off the mortgage and abide with her man until death doth them part.

Chapter Seven
Having my Days in Court

Although the court is supposed to exist so that the truth may be discerned and justice may be dispatched, throughout my career I've viewed the courtroom as a place that is run by and for the lawyers who live and breathe in it. The defendant is the guest of dishonor and the rest of us are merely invited guests and bit players in the dramatic event.

The attorneys are the dancers, and the courtroom is a ballroom in which those learned of the law pirouette, dosey doe, and take their bows. I confess to not having kept a detailed account of all the times I've appeared in court, but I estimate that I've been asked to testify on more than a hundred occasions. Most of the time, the call has come from the prosecution, although periodically – as in the case of the gangland baby killer described above and the one discussed below – I've popped up on behalf of the defense.

On all but one occasion (when I was hauled into the witness box to confirm that a probationer really hadn't shown up for his appointment with me, and that a finding of breach of probation therefore was justified), my presence in the courtroom has been in the capacity of a so-called expert witness.

Each time the attorney who is calling a professional witness wants to have that person qualified as an expert, the court must be satisfied, in a *voir dire* (essentially, a mini trial within the main trial), that the alleged expert truly possesses the requisite expertise. As such, each separate appearance in court is a new beginning, however many times one has been qualified previously.

I've never not been qualified, but sometimes the qualifying process has taken a half an hour or so, during which time the lawyers have waded through my curriculum vitae, and I've had to respond to their questions about my resume, training, and experience. Not a big deal but always a touch tedious and not always entirely pleasant.

Although I believe that for the most part I've performed fairly well when offering my opinion to the court, being in the witness box and being peppered with questions from one side (direct examination), the other side (cross-examination), the first side again (re-direct) and finally the judge, can give credence to the old definition of an 'expert' being 'a drip under pressure'.

In the following pages, I'll outline just a few of the cases that landed me in court, and which linger in my mind. As I do so, I humbly request your understanding. And your compassion.

The business end of a modern court room

Church Bans

During the initial stages of my career, while I was still hungry enough to need the work and naïve enough to think that I could do it without too much risk my ego and professional license, I conducted what are known as custody and access (C&A) assessments.

In those days I did the C&A evaluations for a government agency – which is infinitely preferable to being retained by one parent or the other, but still a risky area of practice. Basically, in custody and access cases, which are renowned as being the area of clinical practice that generates the most complaints to the regulatory college, (invariably the psychologist's opinion is going to annoy one side or the other, and sometimes both) the psychologist interviews and tests all members of the dissolving or recently dissolved family.

The clinician then provides recommendations as to which parent would be preferable as the primary custodian of the children as well as factors such as access to the children by the non-custodial parent. In ideal circumstances, there may be some sort of shared custody arrangements. But that ideal can be difficult to attain, especially when the parents have become embittered and antagonistic toward one another. See the above discussion regarding love turning to hate.

I saw a fair number of families during the couple of years that I poked my head into the lion's jaw of C&A evaluations, sometimes at a pace which, on the rare occasions that I reflect upon it, startles me.

But one file that stands out in my mind involved a post-marital dispute that ended up being a landmark case that was appealed to the highest court in the land.

By the time I got involved in this messy matter, the parents had separated and were in the process of divorcing. As is often the case, Mother (Jill) had been awarded custody of the children, but Father (Jake) had been granted interim access to the kids for one day a week and one weekend a month.

Central to the Jake and Jill dispute was the fact that on one of his access days the dad wanted to take his two prepubescent children to the services that were held by his religious group. Not being of Jake's faith and not wanting the kids to belong to that faith either (or on some level below that, not wanting the children to see too much of Dad), Mom was adamantly opposed to the children attending those meetings. Intensifying the pressure in this case was the fact that the international governing body of the huge religious organization in question correctly interpreted the matter as being a test case that was likely to establish a precedent for similar events and applications.

That being the case, the organization elected to invest a significant amount of resources (underwriting Jake's voluminous legal expenses) to ensure that the decision was favorable to their cause and that Jake was granted official sanction to take his children to his church meetings. I found myself firmly in the middle of this marital dispute when the government agency to which I was consulting referred the case to me for my opinion on the merits of Jake taking the kids to his church.

To try to get my bearings in this explosive access case, I met with Jake and his children both separately and as a group. In addition, and very importantly, I interviewed Jill to canvass her views on the matter and to determine whether her objections were based on the well-being of the children or whether they flowed from her acrimoniousness toward Jake. Or both.

Although Jake seemed like a reasonably pleasant and benign guy, the children were clearly opposed to attending their father's church meetings. In my estimation the kids were sufficiently bright and mature as to be able to make up their own minds on the issue. As such, I formed the opinion that significant credence should be given to their wishes when it came to their church attendance.

Taking everyone's views into consideration and attempting (as always should be the case in any C&A matter, but not always is) to put the best interests of the children ahead of all other considerations, I wrote a report in which I concluded that the kids shouldn't be forced to go to church with their dad if they were disinclined to do so.

My opinion did not go over particularly well with the religious organization, which made it clear that they intended to pursue the matter vigorously. Letters flew back and forth, and I received one from Jake's (i.e. the denomination's) legal representatives demanding that I be deposed by them (that is, attend a formal deposition hearing in which my oral evidence would be recorded) and that I be required to re-evaluate the children.

A year after my initial meeting with the family, but only two weeks before the matter was scheduled to go to trial, the dad's lawyers finally managed to persuade the court to order me to prepare an updated report on the children, primarily to establish whether my opinion had changed from the one I'd conveyed in my earlier report. It had not, and the trial went ahead.

A week or so had been set aside for the court hearing, which was being held in the state's supreme court, and a stellar team of top-notch and very self-important lawyers and their bustling and equally self-important paralegals was flown in from a large, filmy metropolitan area located in a large, leftist southwestern state to represent the father and his religious group.

In light of the fact that my report had been written on behalf of a government agency, and my opinion (unlike the psychologist who had been retained by the religious body, who was a member of that denomination) was as objective and unbiased as I could make it, and despite the fact that the Stellar Legal Team's primary mission was to undermine my evidence, I naively considered the arrayed legal army to be of interest but not too much concern.

However, my concerns – alongside my levels of irritability and blood pressure – were amplified when the Stellar Legal Team tried to intimidate me by persuading a relatively junior officer of the court (interestingly, not the judge who was going to be hearing the case) to issue an order which, among other things, demanded: 1) a list of the memberships, professional organizations and societies to which I belonged; 2) details of my participation as an officer or board member in other organizations; 3) a list of my home and office subscriptions; and 4) a list of all of the psychological text/reference books that I owned. Yikes. Things were beginning to heat up.

Subpoenas being what they are, and defying or ignoring them being an arrestable offense, I complied with the request and a few days later obediently showed up in the courtroom, lists in hand. However, after I'd been sworn in, the first thing I did on the stand was to advise the honorable presiding judge that I wished to contest the obviously vexatious aspects of the order I'd received from the Stellar Legal Team.

This proved to be a satisfying and successful ploy, because the judge, recognizing the contents of the subpoena for what they were, proceeded to excoriate the Stellar Legal Team's lead attorney. Not only did this quash the subpoena, it also unsettled the team's senior lawyer – and by extension the other members of his team – quite nicely and set the tone for the ensuing examination.

I must hand it to those church's lawyers. Unlike the mother's lawyer, who came equipped with himself and a very nice hairstyle, the Stellar Legal Team was at least a half a dozen lawyers strong, several of whom had arrived in court sporting laptops and thick black binders in which they'd tucked away all sorts of research material with which to buttress their case.

I recall that at one point their examining attorney asked me a question about a hypothesis that had been proposed by Anna Freud (daughter of Sigmund and a renowned psychoanalyst in her own right), which I fielded by mumbling something along the lines that "all kinds of things have been hypothesized, but few things have been proven". Considering the amount of the church's cash that the Stellar Legal Team would have been hoovering up per hour, I was generally unimpressed by their overall performance.

But perhaps it was simply that they were swimming upstream, swooping in from outside the state and trying to contest opinions that had been put forward by someone who was consulting on behalf of the government and had no agenda. At the end of the trial, and despite its huge outlay of effort and resources, the judgment went against the religious organization, and it was decreed that Jake couldn't oblige his children to go to church meetings with him.

Nothing against Jake, but particularly given his attorneys' pompous bullying, the decision gave me feelings of vindication and satisfaction.

To no one's surprise, the verdict was appealed by the religious body, and the case was duly reviewed by the regional appellate court. A year or so after the first court judgment, the appeal court agreed with the lower court and upheld the latter's decision. Money not being a problem for the church, and the matter being of major importance to them, they again filed an appeal. And so it came to pass that a few years later the case was heard by the federal supreme court.

In the nation's highest court, my opinion and testimony were cited as factors which had informed the highest court's decision that indeed Jake's children should not be required to go to church with him. And the verdict set a precedent for any future similar scenarios – which was why the religious organization had gone to such lengths to support and argue Jake's case.

Clearly not in the best interests of the church, but in my opinion in the best interests of the children.

Lessons Learned

About five years into my forensic career, a defense attorney for whom I'd previously done some work asked me to speak with one of his clients, Michael. Well, I've been known to say that I believe that the best lessons in life often are the hardest ones. If indeed that is true, Michael and his lawyer certainly were great teachers.

Without becoming overly philosophical or whimsical about how and what I learned from Michael's case, please allow me to share a little about how it all went down. And took me with it.

Michael had been charged with breaking and entering with intent to commit an indictable offense, or something like that. When our paths crossed, he was in pre-trial detention, awaiting trial.

His attorney asked me to conduct a pre-adjudication assessment on Michael, with a specific focus on factors pertaining to why Michael had behaved as he had and – defense lawyers being what they are – whether there was a viable path toward exoneration or, failing that, mitigation. (Or in plain speak, can we make it disappear or at least make it smaller?)

Michael was a slim, fair-haired guy in his late twenties. At first (and second) blush, he came across as a bit of a cool customer. Despite being aloof and detached emotionally, he was quite sane in the sense that he was in good contact with what we consider to be objective reality.

He spoke of his bewilderment as to why he'd engaged in the behavior that had resulted in his charges. He was a qualified commercial pilot with no prior criminal record, and seemingly his alleged felonious actions were quite out of character for him. In short, Michael stood accused of having taken it upon himself to shimmy up to a female neighbor's second-floor condominium, and once there to try to gain entry to her residence.

He had in fact successfully accomplished this somewhat daring aerobatic act, only to have the neighbor spot his surreptitious shimmying and put in a call to the police. At which point Michael had found himself snared dead to rights, caught red-handed and quite possibly (for reasons to be discussed) red-faced.

Given the absence of any similar prior behavior on his part, and his hitherto unblemished personal and professional background, it was of vital interest to establish a motive for Michael's purported malfeasance and once established to assess his risk for repeating such behavior.

Taken at face value, his actions certainly raised the possibility of a sexual or otherwise illicit intent. However, when I interviewed him, he maintained that he had only the fuzziest recollection for the events in question, having been under a great deal of stress at the time and having taken a hefty dose of a prescribed tranquilizer between the time of his arrival home from work and his efforts to gain access to his neighbor's home.

Although even then I wasn't the most trusting of people, he came across as being sincere in his statements and I was somewhat inclined to believe his declarations of befuddlement. In my report to his lawyer, I postulated that at least in part Michael's actions may well have been influenced by his prescription drug use.

Unknown to me at the time, a psychiatrist who also had been retained by the defense attorney had reached a similar conclusion.

It's slightly, but not greatly, comforting to know that I wasn't the only doofus in the dock…

Michael's lawyer ran full-speed with this medication-related motivation, which he said corresponded with his own preconceived notions about what had occurred and offered a plausible explanation and defense for his client's actions.

Basically, the defensive argument being that Michael was not culpable because he had been in a drugged state at the time of the alleged offense and had not formed an intent to commit a crime. Given this strategy, as well as the potential seriousness of the alleged offense, several days were set aside for the trial, on one of which I was scheduled to testify.

I can't recall whether I'd simply consented to furnish testimony regarding my report or whether I had been subpoenaed to do so. But I certainly do remember (despite my very best efforts to repress such traumatic memories) having found myself in the witness box, being examined and cross-examined.

The prosecuting attorney, who was channeling a pit bull during the procedure, was assisted by a psychiatrist whom he'd retained, who sat in the front row of the courtroom as I testified, busily taking notes. And smirking. No pressure whatsoever. All went well during direct examination, during which Michael's lawyer led me through a recitation of my clinical observations and conclusions.

My collar began to feel a size smaller and my brow a couple of degrees hotter, however, when during cross-examination the prosecution revealed information which hitherto had been unknown to me: namely, that Michael had been wearing gloves, a mask, and pantyhose during his ascent to his neighbor's residence – such garments clearly being indicative of a pre-meditated effort to avoid identification by means of facial, fingerprint, and/or DNA recognition.

My bad for having relied on the lawyer and Michael to disclose all the relevant information, and clearly only having had access to a redacted version of the police report. Sloppiness on my part for which I was now paying the price with palpitations and perspiration.

Armed belatedly with such information, the hypothesis that Michael had been significantly impaired by prescription drug use quickly became indefensible. And despite my very best efforts to maintain my courtroom cool as the prosecutor undermined my central thesis – and as his hired-gun psychiatrist leered from the front row – my underarm deodorant was put to the test.

After a couple of hours of blistering cross-examination, it finally and thankfully was over. And with my blood pressure also being way over normal limits, it was high time for the defense attorney to re-establish his case – and my shredded ego and reputation – via re-direct examination. I gazed meekly yet hopefully from the witness box. At which point the defense lawyer stood, composed himself and loudly pronounced that he had "No further questions, Your Honor."

Such was my redemption, or more precisely lack thereof. Mercifully, the judge had no questions for me, and I was dismissed. I scuttled out of that courtroom faster than a willy wilts at an annual polar plunge.

And it provided little solace when I later learned that the psychiatrist who had been retained by the defense had been similarly mauled by the prosecution during cross-examination.

Michael was found guilty without the mitigating factor of drug-induced delirium. By then it was evident, even to me, that he'd deliberately and methodically planned to break into his neighbor's condominium to sexually assault her.

Some time later, I declined the defense lawyer's request to assess another of his clients, and thankfully I never heard from him again. I believe that he might have gone into the insurance business.

But after a few years and with the benefit of hindsight, I became grateful to that attorney for the lessons that he'd unwittingly provided: namely, that in order to prepare satisfactorily for a case, it was incumbent upon me to ensure that I had all available relevant reports made available to me prior to embarking upon an assessment, and that I not be influenced, consciously or unconsciously, by the retaining party. Sloppiness, laziness, and bias are never good companions in the witness box.

Striving for an absence of bias is crucial because even though professionals are ethically and legally bound to provide impartial reports and evidence, in my experience there's no doubt that some clinicians who've been retained and paid by the defense are inclined take a relatively lenient view of the offender, whereas those who've been retained by the prosecution or the court tend to be more severe in their evaluations.

In many instances this propensity may operate on an unconscious level, and therefore it's something that needs to be checked and rechecked on an ongoing basis by every examining clinician. Ever since my experience with Michael, I've performed such mental checks much more vigorously, and I believe that I became a better – and humbler – forensic psychologist because of it.

I'd therefore like to think that I'm grateful to Michael and his lawyer for having made me undergo my own trial by fire. Yes, I certainly would like to think that….

Sagging Male, Soaring Female

I originally saw Sam on behalf of his supervising probation officer. The officer in question was seeking my opinion about Sam's overall psychological status, risk factors, and case management needs. Sam had FASD (Fetal Alcohol Spectrum Disorder), and he exhibited some of its negative effects in the form of limitations of intelligence, motivation, and physical condition.

Indeed, some may say that Sam was a weedy and inept kind of guy, unlikely to have been a hit at his local pick-up bar. Of course, there was also the small matter of his sexual interest in children, which in addition to his overall unattractiveness to adult women was one of the reasons why he'd sexually offended against a child, been jailed, and at the time of our first meeting was on probation.

(From a causal perspective, it's entirely possible that Sam initially gravitated toward children to meet his sexual needs because in many respects he was childlike himself and because he was unable to attract an age-appropriate partner. He may also simply have been preferentially attracted to the undeveloped child's body type.)

I conducted a routine clinical interview of Sam, gave him a couple of psychological tests, and prepared a relatively brief report for his probation officer. I advised that Sam was at risk for future problems and should be monitored accordingly. I didn't give Sam another thought.

Then, several years later a subpoena came my way, directing me to testify at a dangerous offender hearing in which Sam was to be the headline attraction. Apparently, after I saw him, Sam had continued to commit sexual crimes. In fact, his sexual criminality had been so consistent and significant that the prosecution services were attempting to have him declared a dangerous offender and to have him given an indeterminate or indefinite prison sentence.

I recall two memorable things about Sam's dangerous offender hearing. The first was Sam himself: he hadn't grown any more burly or attractive since our meeting several years earlier. He also continued to exude the same lack of interest and motivation that had characterized him during our previous encounter. Frankly, he seemed to be – and almost certainly was – utterly bored by the proceedings.

I remember thinking then, as I had when I'd seen him before, how Sam really hadn't been put together very well physically or mentally: not only did he have a few facial characteristics of FASD, but he also had a gauntness and awkwardness to him that rendered him singularly unappealing. He lolled in his chair as if he was about to fall out of it, and at one point when I was providing my testimony, he was either asleep or resolutely resting his eyes.

Mrs. Manson has been known to say that I have that effect on some people, but in a courtroom, he should have been able to at least feign awareness, especially when it was his neck that was on the line.

The second memorable aspect to the hearing was that, apart from the defendant and guests such as me, it was an all-girl extravaganza. There was a female judge, a female prosecutor, a female defense attorney, a female court transcriber, and even a pistol-packing female guard. It occurred to me then, as it does now, that the situation was a metaphor for the ascendancy (and some might say revenge) of the female in the western world, with an all-woman cast of players judging whether this male miscreant was sufficiently dangerous that he should spend many or most of his remaining days behind bars.

The odds certainly were not in Sam's favor. Maybe he knew this, which was why he was so disinterested and sleepy and detached from it all, evidently just wanting to get back to the comforts of his cell. (By the way, a lot of incarcerated guys fall ill while attending court: the long drive to and from jail, the lengthy and often stressful days in the courtroom, and the lunches that often consist of little more than a sandwich can be wearing and conducive to sickness.)

As expected, Sam was indeed declared a dangerous offender, thereby providing him with the opportunity to enjoy the perks of prison for the foreseeable future. Particularly for a guy with Sam's lassitude and below-average intelligence, if ever he were to be released from custody, he would have considerable difficulty adjusting to life in the community. In fact, I suspect that by the time he was declared a dangerous offender he'd already grown very accustomed to an incarcerated and rule-bound lifestyle, in which almost all the decisions were made for him, all of the meals and furnishings provided, and the social demands relatively limited.

Such institutionalization is quite common among those who are confined to places such as prisons for any length of time, and in some people it can begin to set in even during relatively short sentences. Given Sam's basic lack of competency to meet the challenges of the modern world, he would have been highly susceptible to the rapid onset of institutionalization.

Outside of jail, should he ever get there, he would be at grave risk for total dependency upon government and charitable support, petty criminality, and a speedy descent into substance abuse and homelessness. Poor Sam didn't have much going for him when I saw him in the courtroom, and I wouldn't be at all surprised to learn that now, over 20 years later, he's dead. No matter how much we may aspire for equity, equality and fairness in life, it is not and never will be fair or equal in this fallible field of existence.

And some, like Sam exemplify that sad and harsh reality.

A Decidedly Disagreeable Dangerous Offender

It was in the early days of my career that I endured my first encounter with Omar. I had a memorable meeting with him in a probation office that specialized in the supervision of sex offenders. Omar had behaved in a sexually inappropriate fashion with a young woman – following her, pushing her up against a wall, and undoing her brassiere.

Which I suppose wouldn't necessarily have been a bad thing, had the woman invited his amorous overtures and had known him beforehand, but she didn't and hadn't. Because of his unsolicited and unsavory behavior Omar had been convicted of sexual assault and had served close to a 2-year prison sentence. When I met him, he was on probation.

Omar was showing himself to be a difficult supervision client, and I was called upon to provide an opinion regarding his personality, mental status, risk factors, suitability for treatment, and overall case management.

It would be something of an understatement to say that my rendezvous with Omar went well. From the outset of the interview, he came across in a resistant, supercilious, and disdainful manner, pointedly refusing to acknowledge me as anyone worthy of his time and attention. In turn, my ego rose uproariously to the occasion, and I became terse and testy right back at him.

Apparently, he'd been informed by his 'treating' psychiatrist (that is, someone who was being paid by the state to provide him with unstructured and likely useless counseling, supposedly to reduce his risk of re-offense) that there was no need for him to cooperate with me. Such is the reality of professional egos and territoriality – the psychiatrist in question, who had a reputation with which I was familiar, clearly had his own personality and ego issues with which to deal, as well as an axe to grind. (But he died before getting old, so I won't think or speak too badly of him.)

At any rate, during our encounter Omar brandished a pad of paper on which he pointedly wrote down all my questions. He also exhibited tempestuousness and a short temper, at one point taking some items from his pocket and angrily and violently throwing them on the table after becoming particularly piqued at something that I'd said.

As an aside, most of my meetings with the people I assessed, including even the most hardened offenders, went quite well. Although most of the individuals I evaluated for the government weren't delighted about having to undergo a psych assessment, in the main they went through the motions in a cooperative and polite manner.

They were aware of my role and more generally as previously mentioned they recognized that it was in their best interests to go along with the process and pretend to get along with the evaluator - especially if they had an interest (parole; early release; reduced sentence) in doing so. In return, I always tried to be respectful and affable with the people who were undergoing assessment, and I believe I had something of a knack for reading them and matching or 'pacing' their personal style.

But Omar was an entirely different kettle of fish. Evidently adhering to the dictates and vagaries of his personality as well as the extremely dubious advice of his psychiatrist, Omar was unpleasantly condescending and uncooperative.

After our meeting I relied upon Omar's presentation, offense dynamics, and file information to cobble together a hopefully useful and balanced report for the referring probation officer. In a nutshell, I conveyed my opinion that Omar was "impoverished" in his capacity to manage his impulses, was highly uninsightful, had a low tolerance for stress and frustration, and was a very angry man.

I considered him to have a "very modest" ability to contemplate or worry about the effects that his actions had on others. His offense signified an incapacity to control his sexual impulses, feelings of entitlement and misogyny, and a complete disregard and lack of empathy for his victim.

All of this despite his previous participation in a variety of forms of counseling and treatment, and his ongoing 'therapeutic' relationship with a psychiatrist. I opined that Omar was one hostile hombre who represented a continuing behavioral risk. I was unlikely to rise to the very top of Omar's Christmas card list after he read my report. Indeed, on the contrary, I later learned that he blamed me and my report for his subsequent difficulties in life. Some people have no appreciation or respect!

As Mrs. Manson would be among the very first to tell you, I am a person who is extremely reluctant to say "I told you so" – unless of course, I did tell you so and occasionally if I did not. And in this case, I did tell them so. While he was on probation, Omar proved to be a constant challenge to supervise, and nothing meaningful seems to have been accomplished by virtue of his supervision or supposed treatment.

Omar went on to become a repeat sex offender. He also experienced troubles on the home front, and at one point he was convicted of assaulting and harassing his estranged wife. This was hardly surprising. What did attract my attention and interest was that as noted above, Omar attributed his domestic disharmony and other troubles to me, claiming that in some mysterious way my report about him had brought about the ruination of his marriage.

And so it was that about eleven years later, Omar and I had the pleasure of seeing each other again. On our second encounter, I observed him from a supreme court witness box, adjacent to which Omar sat and fulminated in the prisoner's box.

We'd been reunited within the context of an application that had been brought forward by the government to have Omar declared a 'sexual assault dangerous offender'. He was thus in peril of receiving an indeterminate sentence.

I still have the transcript of my testimony at that hearing, which I believe for some reason was sent to me by the prosecutor's office. The transcript and my recollection seem to suggest that my role in the proceedings went reasonably well, a particularly memorable moment having come when Omar's vocalizations and gesticulations of anger at something I had said during my testimony had required the intervention of his attorney to try to get him to settle down.

He hadn't changed a bit.

At least, not for the better.

In one line of questioning during my oral evidence, Omar's lawyer, who was a senior attorney of some renown, attempted to imply that Omar's behavior toward women could have been attributed to his ethnicity and/or to cultural factors. His gambit didn't gain traction (sexual assault and assaultive behavior generally being frowned upon in all civilized societies, despite the residual prevalence of patriarchal and misogynistic views in some parts of the world), and at the conclusion of the proceedings the court decided that Omar satisfied the criteria for a dangerous offender.

In my opinion, a wise judgment. Omar is one of the few guys I would not want to meet again one fine day – say, while I'm whistling a lively tune as I wash and wax Mrs. Manson's car – because his mixture of hostility, weirdness, impulsivity, lack of insight, projection of blame, and proven inability to control his aggressiveness, made for an unwholesome and volatile mixture.

I would not be at all keen to rekindle my acquaintance with Omar – and I expect and hope that he feels the same way about me.

Long-Term Pain

Being designated a dangerous or long-term offender isn't likely to turn a guy into a major babe magnet – although as I mentioned earlier there's no accounting for taste and a certain kind of woman finds dangerous men alluring. In addition, such designation can generate a lengthy and even indeterminate sentence, which severely curtails one's opportunities for cruising the bars.

The following account is presented as a brief illustration of how much time and effort can go into having someone designated a long-term, dangerous, or prolific offender. Unfortunately, sometimes such efforts provided only a marginal enhancement of public safety.

Anton was a sex offender in his early thirties who since the age of twelve had accrued a lengthy criminal history. He'd targeted children during several sexual offenses and had incorporated violence and threats of violence into some of those felonies. When he was sixteen Anton raped a 7-year-old girl.

Later, he moved up the age scary scale when he raped, at knifepoint, a 14-year-old girl. He spent several years in jail and at least twice he refused to participate in custodial sex offender treatment programs. Ironically, while attending sex offender treatment in the community, he'd re-offended by making multiple indecent telephone calls (which were quite common until technology in the form of call display and call tracing put most of the indecent callers out of business). He also managed to escape police custody.

Anton had been diagnosed with pedophilia, transvestic fetishism, telephone scatalogia (obscene phone calling), alcohol dependence, and antisocial personality. When I assessed him, he was on probation but, understandably enough, his probation officer was very concerned about his stability and risk levels.

Anton assured me that his sexually deviant thinking and behavior were in the past, and that he was no longer troubled by thoughts and fantasies related to children and forcible intercourse (aka rape). Despite such professed progress, Anton said that he did need to talk to me about issues pertaining to his sexuality. Specifically, he noted that he'd been cross-dressing since he was about seven years of age and that (despite having offended against females) he was attracted primarily to males.

He even claimed that although females had picked on him for much of his life, he'd been contemplating undergoing reconstructive surgery, with the intention of transitioning to a female. Anton also wanted to discuss why it took him so long to reach orgasm.

Undoubtedly, had I pursued that line of chit chat, it would have been more than enough to keep the therapeutic conversation going for quite some time and to fill quite a few notepads.

So, what's an assessing forensic psychologist to do? Engage Anton in a warm, cozy and meaningful, healing discussion about his seemingly convoluted sexuality? Or pursue a more pragmatic and perhaps challenging or confrontative intervention approach?

I chose the latter, querying Anton about his various assertions, based on the premise that his stated wish to talk about his cross-dressing and orgasms, although by no means totally unrelated or necessarily unimportant, was something of a manipulative red herring, designed to divert and consume the allotted assessment time and circumvent discussion of any substantive issues.

During our conversation, Anton grudgingly acknowledged that in fact he did continue to be sexually attracted to female adolescents. But when I asked him whether he would be willing to undergo an objective evaluation of sexual interest he demurred.

Examination of Anton's mental state revealed that he was free from any significant mental disorder and was of approximately average intelligence. However, my opinion at the time was that he had an antisocial personality and was likely to be impulsive, sensation-seeking, easily frustrated, conflicted, hostile and rebellious.

A prevailing self-focus, moodiness, and resistance to authority also were probable. I rated him as being significantly psychopathic and as being at moderate-to-high risk for sexual recidivism. Psychological testing supported my clinical impressions, interpretation of the test results suggesting that he was likely to be manipulative, demanding, impulsive, immature, narcissistic, hostile, irritable, emotionally labile, dissatisfied, and all in all a difficult person with whom to get along.

In addition to such personality features, my conclusion that Anton was at elevated risk for engaging in future sex offending was predicated on factors such as his penchant for substance use and his potential to experience a perilous mixture of boredom, low mood and sexual frustration.

I also believed him to be trying to divert attention away from salient offending issues by trying to discuss matters such as cross-dressing and delayed orgasms.

Certainly, he was an eclectically confused fellow when it came to his sexuality, but focusing on those areas to the exclusion of core relapse prevention variables would not have been appropriate. I didn't consider him to be interested in, or at that time likely to benefit from, routine sex offender treatment – in large part because he'd never truly shown an interest in such treatment and because a focus upon deviant sexuality during treatment could have served to trigger and exacerbate his aberrant thinking and behavior.

In my recommendations I also made a number of other proposals, such as objective sexual interest testing, avoidance or at least minimization of alcohol and drug use (always easier to recommend than to implement, at least on a sustained basis), and the prescription of an antidepressant medication with anti-obsessive properties.

However, I didn't consider Anton to be likely to want to take such medication, and I saw him as being even less likely to be enthusiastic about taking anti-androgen medication – however useful such a drug could have been in lowering his potential to act upon his problematic sexual urges.

All things considered, Anton would appear to have been an excellent candidate for a long-term or dangerous offender designation, and indeed my written reports on him, and my oral testimony at his court hearing, may have gone some way toward such a judicial finding.

At his hearing, I testified that Anton's risk for violent sexual aggressiveness was likely to decline only as he aged, and that even then his potential for engaging in sexual activity with children probably would remain a problem for quite some time.

Following the submission of my evidence and the testimony of other expert witnesses, and strong prosecutorial argument, Anton was indeed designated a long-term offender but to my astonishment was given a relatively paltry 3-year sentence.

The safety net, such as it was, being that the prison sentence was to be followed by ten years of community supervision.

Accordingly, Anton was packed off to the penitentiary to serve his sentence. A few years later, he was back in his home community, the tab for his board and room being picked up by the government on account of the safeguarding stipulation that he had to reside in a corrections halfway house.

A couple of months after that, he was arrested for having breached some of his parole conditions. During his arrest, he fled from the police but was re-apprehended and sentenced to another year in jail. Upon his release, he was returned to a halfway house, still under his 10-year supervision order.

Shortly afterwards, he absconded again, and following recapture he was given yet another year's imprisonment.

The most recent information I have on Anton is that he had once again been ordered to reside in a halfway house, his various escapades and elopements having resulted in an extension of his original supervision order.

Not exactly what might be seen as a success story, but I guess if his subsequent offending was confined to escaping lawful custody and not raping anyone else, this would be something of a success for someone with Anton's disposition.

And for Anton and those of his ilk, success must be measured in terms of them just growing older without engaging in significant sexual or violent reoffending. The reality being that, as I've repeatedly mentioned, the risk for a vast majority of such serious offenders only declines meaningfully as they burn-out, their sexually aggressive drive diminishes, and they mellow and glide into their golden years.

Chapter Eight
Crystal Ball & Navel Gazing

Gazing back mistily upon the bygone days of my career in criminality, it sometimes comes as a bit of a surprise to me that I lasted for as long as I did in the fetid forensic trenches. During my training and in the earlier stages of my vocation, it was often opined that the career lifespan of a forensic psychologist was about ten years, after which the high-flying shrink usually stumbled off into staider but far less stressful areas of practice or clinical administration.

Specialization in forensic assessments is a high-pressure business in which the performance demands, consequences – to the lives of others, to the professional involved, and to society as a whole – are significant.

However, just like porn stars, some have more staying power and firmness than others, and don't allow what I call the 'creep seep' (the seeping into one's psyche of some of the negativity associated with dealing with dark, damaged, and damaging individuals and their crimes) get to them too quickly. A touch of psychopathy helps a person to stay in the game, serving as it does as a shield with which to ward off, or at least to slow down, the penetration of the nasty stuff.

Also, things have changed a bit since I kicked off my career.

One such change was discussed above – namely, that there has been an increased reliance on testing and various other scoring measures with which to more accurately, or at least more objectively and safely, appraise risk.

Another change has been wrought by reductions in and modifications to the health care insurance industry in the United States, which has prompted more psychologists to turn to forensic work as a means of making a buck. Back in the day, I was one of a handful of psychologists who was willing to put his (in those days there were very few females doing forensic work) reputation on the line and see the kinds of people, and make (and sometimes defend in court) the kinds of decisions that were required of the forensic psychologist.

Today there are many more shrinks trying to squeeze a living out of the misery industries of crime and its close relations law enforcement, detention, and correction.

During the past few decades, the field of psychology, like medicine and law, also has witnessed a major demographic change. As with most professions, psychology used to be male dominated. Now it is, quite dramatically, female dominated.

Such dominance recently was reflected and epitomized by an article that was produced and published by the American Psychological Association (APA), in which traditional masculinity was decried and derided as being unhealthy and unhelpful.

Although I won't delve into the merits of the APA's argument, which would be akin to having a couple of drinks and then immersing oneself in a hearty discussion about religion and politics with a burly bunch of tattooed and armed strangers, I would merely query whether the APA ever would dream of publishing an analogous piece, penned by men, on the deleterious aspects of traditional femininity or the sinister side of radical feminism.

Males and masculinity have taken quite a beating during the past forty or so years. Western men in their twenties and even thirties have known nothing but a world in which females have been depicted as the victims of men but who at the same time are somehow morally better, wiser, and even stronger than their male counterparts. Maleness, on the other hand, has been portrayed as being synonymous with badness or at best silliness.

And although I would agree that – as attested to by the accounts in this work – some males can behave very badly and very toxically indeed, those individuals represent only a very small percentage of the total male population. To tarnish all boys and men with that badness is fashionable but unfortunate.

There is no doubt that things are going a bit squirrelly in our world, and that men, who in the main have been the politicians and generals at the helm, must bear their share of the responsibility for these troubled times.

Also, it can be argued that in times of stress – and make no mistake, these were stressful times even before the Coronavirus pandemic made the entire world freak out – there can be a perceived need to identify and vilify a causal factor or scapegoat. For several reasons, including the fact that in a society in which physical labor and daily household protection are no longer believed to be as necessary as they used to be, males have been both justifiably and unjustifiably targeted.

Males always have been the more disposable gender (wars, industrial accidents, accidental overdoses, and suicides being among the prime ways with which males prematurely shuck off their mortal coils), but in recent decades the failings, superfluity and disposability of the male sex has been more explicitly debated and promulgated within the traditional and social media.

We are witnessing the results of the denigration of males. Boys are falling behind academically, men comprise about 80 percent of the drug overdoses and a vast majority of the homelessness that increasingly pervades North American and European streets, and males take their lives by suicide at rates three to four times those of females.

Although there has been an increasing awareness of such male health factors, it will be a little longer before the societal effects of such masculine descendancy really hit home. Or, until a large scale or cataclysmic event occurs, causing 'traditional masculine' skills such as capability, physical strength, ingenuity and constructiveness again to be considered valuable and indeed invaluable.

Regardless, the psychology field, like medicine and law and the media, has become quite feminized. No heavy lifting or dirty fingernails required. Coincident with this, mental health rivals to professional psychology have arisen.

Such rivalry has come primarily from so-called registered clinical counselors as well as from some social workers and a diverse group of people who lay claim to being able to counsel others. Without debating the qualifications or qualities of such supposed sources of succor and support, I'll simply note that counselors have replaced psychologists in a number of fields of professional endeavor, especially in those areas which provide short-term counseling, treatment and even assessment in agencies such as corrections, workers compensation, and employee assistance programs.

In large part, such change has been inspired by budgetary considerations: counselors are cheaper than qualified psychologists. Although the psychological governing and licensing bodies have managed to protect their turf (under the justifiable guise of protecting the public) by restricting functions such as diagnosis to clinical psychology and medicine, leaks have sprung in this defensive dyke.

In fact, to some extent such pressures on psychology have flowed directly or indirectly from the very agency that is tasked with protecting the public – that is, the government – which itself has shown an unseemly interest in employing lesser-qualified but alluringly lower-paid counselors.

It will be interesting to see how all of this plays out. I must say, however, that at some point western society's understandable and in some ways laudably passionate interest in trauma, victims, victimization, healing, triggering, safe spaces and all-things sensitive is likely to grow a little jaded and stale.

This could come about abruptly – recall the sudden change in focus after the 2020 pandemic struck and in a more general sense consider the effects of any sudden catastrophic event, especially one that cuts off the consumables supply chain. The angst of one's inner child tends not to be quite so compelling when the sky is falling, and the buildings are burning.

Or the change could come more gradually, as the pendulum inexorably swings back toward the middle. Balance being something for which most of us strive but seldom attain.

If I were asked to bet on what will happen, I'd be inclined to prognosticate that (despite the presence of some highly evolved beings in the world right now, usually but not always manifesting as spiritual teachers of one form or another) some sort of nasty incident will occur that will remind us that, despite all of the luxurious conveniences we enjoy in our modern first-world civilization, we're really just squatting atop an illusion.

The COVID-19 pandemic panic gave us a taste of that, but I suspect that in certain respects it may only have been an appetizer for the main course. Underneath this illusory cushion of modern comfort and convenience lies the rock-hard reality that we're biological beings who at any given time are about 4 weeks away from death without food, 3 or 4 days away from death without water, and around 6 to 10 minutes away from death without oxygen.

At this very moment, our lives are precariously maintained entirely by the ingredients that are provided to us by nature. And by the technological wonders that convey those resources to us. How do we fare when we experience even a brief power outage? How do we feel when we have no water flowing from our taps or hot water gushing from our showers? How do we manage when our cellular and internet services goes down?

What would we do, and how would we feel, if such amenities were to go away and stay away? How would we access the money with which to buy food and water if all internet services were inoperative, and the ATMs and even online banking records couldn't be accessed? Just a few considerations to remind us that most of us are big, spoiled softies at heart, who wouldn't last more than a few days in a true wilderness situation.

We are irreparably reliant on an ultimately and increasingly fragile technological infrastructure to support and nurture our lives and indulgences. Take away the technology, and for most of us you will take away our life. I would also add to this admittedly pessimistic perspective that, if nothing else, my decades of working with criminals have taught me that if society were to break down – or even crumble a bit around its edges – a certain kind of person would be most favored to assume dominance or control.

In the animal world, such beings tend to be the larger, more aggressive, and usually male individuals who vie for, and assume, a position of dominance. It really isn't that long ago that such physical attributes were directly correlated with human leadership roles, and if we were to scratch away our society's rich and glossy veneer, I suspect that we would quickly see a reversion to such a scenario.

As I noted earlier, there is an adage about people sleeping peacefully in their beds at night only because rough men stand ready to do violence on their behalf. Something for all of us to contemplate – particularly, some might argue, those who lobby for more gun control, less freedom for dissenting speech (while clamoring for their own rights, more diversity, more gender equality more equity, more environmental sensitivity and more apologies for the transgressions wrought by our unenlightened ancestors), and more state care and inherent control over our daily lives: lives that are comfortable, cosseted and increasingly dependent upon a progressively more fractured and indebted state.

And on the touchy subject of gun control, let's pause for a moment to examine the causal factors that are catalyzing our desire to disarm the regular citizens of this fine land (and make no mistake – gun control simply means that ordinary citizens can't have guns –

the military, police, and by extension the political ruling class that is protected by their weapon-carrying guards remain armed, as do any criminals who wish to source such weaponry).

The principal factors fuelling such a disarmament momentum are a fear of the violence wrought by criminal gangs and acts of terrorism. Stereotypes and hype to the contrary, the latter is primarily (but certainly not exclusively) domestic and homegrown, exemplified by the mass shootings that began to appear in the 1960s (the University of Texas tower shooting having been one of the first such multiple homicides).

And what is causing the upsurge in such violence and terrorism?

Well, you decide. I would suggest that we are collectively and increasingly becoming more stressed and crazier. Indeed, if we look objectively at our world, it becomes apparent that for some time we've been on a downward, degenerative trajectory into mental and social instability. Arising from such instability is our tendency to feel more anxious, vigilant, and fearful. And in a leap of simplistic logic, we reason that if we take away the exploding tools of violence, we will make ourselves safe again, and pacify the world and therefore our minds.

As alluring as such a course of action sounds, it won't work – at least not without taking away the causal factors underlying, for example, the horrid and cruel mass shootings. But for a little while it might make some people feel better and make them believe that they are doing their bit for world or personal peace. And it might get some politicians elected.

Still, if we can't go to a nightclub or a mall without having some nagging thought that an active shooting or bombing or knifing or van driving situation could arise, we've arrived at a very dark place in our world.

And also arising as a response to our fearfully nagging concerns about the state of the world has been an increased focus on political correctness and rectitude. We're talking an exceptionally good talk about being better people and righting the wrongs of our ancestors. But have we really changed as human beings?

Having spent many hours inside jails, I might use the analogy of putting a group of angry people in a prison. Impose on the prisoners lots of rules and regulations. The prisoners will tend to behave themselves if they have no alternative to doing so. However, if given an opportunity, as illustrated by the riot in the old prison that was described at the beginning of this book, they will break down the prison fixtures and walls, lash out at their captors and those at the bottom of the inmate hierarchy, and generally give full vent to the furious emotions that in many cases had generated or at least catalyzed their imprisonment.

Similarly, if we imprison our emotions, tamping them down or having them tamped down by social rules and our workplace and social media-inspired fears of being singled out as being incorrect or abhorrent, our emotions won't change for the better, and in fact may become more intense and negative the longer they're held captive by external forces.

Given an opportunity, those emotions will rise to the surface and explode outward, often with unhappy consequences. There is a reason why people 'go postal', and why mass homicide events have become more commonplace. All the human rights rules in the world will not change much in our world until we as human beings intrinsically change.

And by change, I mean genuinely transcend the delusions and negative emotions that govern our perceptions and behavior. The semi-science of psychology can be very entertaining and immensely interesting, and it can do some good if applied correctly. But it should not become a cause unto itself, and feed upon, reflect, and intensify our superficial narcissism and self-focus.

When most of us do not know who we really are, it's difficult for us to change who we are. Or to become truly better, unprejudiced, and kind people. So, hatred, racism, misandry, and misogyny will not diminish simply because society says that they should not be given expression, and that we should be more generous and understanding and diversely equal and inclusive.

Our attachments and emotions merely seek other avenues with which to manifest themselves – by way of the populist movements emerging throughout the world, or by means of the acts of mass violence and destruction.

As humans, we really haven't changed all that much, and although we may like to think otherwise, we're still the same beings who have continuously slaughtered one another, often in the most heinous ways imaginable, since the dawn of humankind. It isn't until we truly transform and understand who we really are and how we're all connected, that we will make genuine progress.

At best, simply to supress our clamoring emotions such as anger, desire and ignorance buys us some time and allows us to feel and behave better temporarily and superficially.

Most of the time, such suppression enables us to talk ourselves into believing that we're fundamentally changing and improving – prattling on about ourselves and our own morality while castigating those with alternative views – when in truth we are just the same old people.

Still, as I started out, so shall I stop. Just as sad and sordid jails can be found amidst the happiest and most serene spots, so can happiness be discovered amidst the chaos of our minds. In the moments between our thoughts can come contentment and insight.

And although our contentment never seems to last, and we are all headed toward the same place, appreciating the moment, and keeping a good sense of humor while we're experiencing the vicissitudes of life and death can help us to keep our sunny sides up.

Trying to enjoy the ride as we seek to work out who we really are and what life is all about.

And following the example of Robert –a young and highly damaged former patient of mine, who when asked how life was going for him would reflexively respond "all right…(long pause)…so far", we can strive to row our boats gently but purposefully down the streaming dream of this life. And merely try do our very best.

Tamam Shud

Mad Manson (pandemic & highway robbery ready)

About the Author

D r. Maddox Manson spent over three decades practising as a forensic psychologist, cavorting with criminals at the request of various government agencies, attorneys, and others. He has assessed thousands of offenders, many of whom were murderers and/or sexual predators.

He resides near a major metropolitan center close to a coast. Finally rebelling against the guidance of his wife's accountant, he recently retired from active practice to devote more time to his online gaming, social media, philanthropic, and oenophiliac commitments.

Dr. Manson's final professional pontification is reputed to have been: "Old forensic psychologists never die; they just shrink a bit more."

9 7 9 8 2 1 8 5 1 9 3 9 1